COHERENT HEART

A HERO'S ODYSSEY

ELEVATING WITH STRENGTH

LALI A. LOVE

Disclaimer

The views and poetry in this book reflect the author's personal experiences and are not intended as medical or psychological advice. The content is not a substitute for professional guidance. The author does not hold a psychology degree and offers no claims regarding mental health treatment. Readers are encouraged to seek appropriate professional help as needed.

Coherent Heart:
A Hero's Odyssey

Distributed by Bublish Inc.

eBook ISBN: 9781647049263
Paperback ISBN: 9781647049249

Award-Winning Publications
Heart of a Warrior Angel: From Darkness to Light (2019)
The Joy of I.T. - Infinite Transcendence (2020)
The De-Coding of Jo 1: Hall of Ignorance (2020)
The De-Coding of Jo 2: Blade of Truth (2021)
The De-Coding of Jo 3: Keys to Eternity (2022)
Organic eMotions: Poetry for hUmaNITY (2022)
Realms of My Soul 3 Book Poetry Series (2023)

Dedication

Welcome to the realms,
Where dreams softly gleam,
Hearts entwine in the simplest scheme.
Fear not the vibes ahead,
With me, dangers shed,
On our swan road,
We'll gather and redeem.

Grand Design

Within the vast expanse of darkened skies,
We are cells adrift in cosmic seas,
Filled with distant stars that gleam and rise,
A dance of light waves, an opus of keys.

Each oscillation brings us near,
A waltz of neurons, we draw together,
In the boundless expanse, we find kinship clear,
In unity, were linked, entwined forever.

Through the ebb and flow of celestial tides,
Our brains, like galaxies, swirl and spin,
Connections forming as the universe guides,
A grand design, where mysteries begin.

We float as one, in this tapestry of grace,
Bound by the rhythms of the cosmic breeze,
Cells and stars converge, a wondrous embrace,
In this boundless expanse, we find our peace.

"When we operate from the space of heart-centered consciousness, every Soul becomes our mirror and our teacher. We are all connected within this harmonic web of pure radiant life force energy called Love."

—Lali A. Love

A seed in the soil, hidden below,
Grows its roots, strong and in tow.
Through the earth, it'll stand,
Rising tall, firm, and grand,
Elevating with strength, in the world's flow.

CONTENTS

FORWARD

In a world of shadows, where doubts take flight,
Confidence falters, lost in fear's cruel plight.
Yet, amidst the chaos, let this truth be clear,
You're a gem of uniqueness, precious and dear.

Let these words caress your weary soul,
In their warmth, find comfort, feel whole.
You're worthy, my friend, let that be your goal,
A treasure beyond measure, a shining pole.

More valuable than gold, you truly are,
With each breath, you shine, like a guiding star.
Your talents and strengths, a beacon afar,
Illuminate the path, wherever you are.

Believe in yourself, let your heart lead the way,
You're capable of more than you dare to say.
Though stumbles may come, and trials may test,
Your inner strength will rise above the rest.

Be gentle with yourself, and cherish your worth,
Put self-care first, as you traverse this earth.

Forgive the past, beloved, let go of the pain,
Embrace the journey, let your spirit reign.

You're a masterpiece in progress, ever-growing,
Through life's twists and turns, keep on flowing.
In harmony and balance, let your Qi energy soar,
Embrace your authenticity and shine like a star.

PART 1

Philosophy of my Soul

INTRODUCTION

Know Thyself

As a reader of my published work, you have likely sensed the deeper, mystical currents running through my stories and poetry. My writing is rooted in a profound understanding of reality, shaped by my metaphysical beliefs in the transformative power of self-actualization. These themes aren't just ideas—they are the very heart of my journey.

Since I began my path of self-discovery, I have realized that wisdom isn't found by "pretending to be positive". True intelligence is uncovered in the practice of gratitude for every moment, no matter how dark or light. It's about feeling deeply and embracing life's richness. This shift in mindset allowed me to reconnect with who I AM, unveiling life's authentic beauty.

When I was a young child, I wrestled with the concept of "God" as presented by religion and society. The notions of hell, fear, guilt, and division never resonated with my spirit.

I couldn't accept the idea of being subservient to a distant, judgmental figure who demanded devotion and punished those who strayed. Something inside me whispered that there was more to existence—something greater, something that didn't require fear to connect with the Creator.

However, in the first seven years of life, I absorbed everything like a sponge, from my environment and parents, shaping how I saw myself and the world. During this formative time, I was conditioned out of my pure nature, taught to believe that I was powerless and at the mercy of external forces.

This belief sculpted my ego-based identity and planted the seeds of my childhood wounds. It slowly pulled me into a cycle of disempowerment, where I relinquished my inner strength and disconnected from my true essence. I was desperate for rescue, but did not buy into the illusion of an external savior.

Throughout my schooling, I often felt like an outsider, longing to belong, to feel safe in my own skin, to be seen and valued for who I was. I craved unconditional love—quirks and all. That yearning to be seen led me to dissociate from my body during traumatic moments, wishing I could escape this earthly plane and return "home."

I have come to realize that the effect of trauma isn't about what happens to us; it's how we internalize that devastating pain as young children. It is a deep emotional wound that results from overwhelming experiences, causing an inflamed nervous system, leaving a lasting impact on our sense of self and ability to cope.

When we abandon our inner child, we start to bypass our *Organic eMotions*, or energy in motion, burying the feelings that need to be expressed. We suppress or push down the very force meant to guide and heal us, dampening its charge. Over time, this self-depression takes a toll, leading to dis-ease—manifesting in autoimmune disorders, mental health struggles, and physical ailments.

Whether it was the emotional fallout from our parents' divorce, our father's alcoholism, physical, psychological, or sexual violence, disfunction or any profound sense of loss—it's not the event itself that defines the trauma, but how it altered our inner world and our identity.

The harm impacted our inner state of being, how those experiences disconnected us from our emotional body, and the present moment. Our souls fragmented, frozen in stagnation, when our inner child felt unsafe and unloved. We went into survival mode, or "offline" from our true being, unable to cope and process the pain. Over time, this internal withdrawal created a distorted view of ourselves, others, and the world around us, harboring distrust.

I have understood that our human emotions are complex psychological and physiological responses to stimuli, reflecting our internal state and external experiences. They serve as a form of communication between the mind and body, influencing thoughts, behaviors, and interactions. They are the raw energy that fuels how we connect, react, and grow, revealing the truth of who we are at every moment.

When we dissociate from the fragmented parts of ourselves, we shut down the very emotions that once demanded to be felt. Fear, sadness, guilt, and anger are muted, replaced by a deep numbness. In this state, we no longer connect to our own heart, becoming distant.

The distress, neglect, or emotional hardship creates this inner divide, where the weight of those experiences feels too heavy to bear.
And so, instead of confronting the pain, we retreat, growing up with an inflamed nervous system, while silently struggling beneath the surface.

As young children, we didn't have the tools to process and heal our emotions from the distressful events, so the negative perspectives linger, showing up repeatedly in our life, even long after the original distressful event occurred.

I have learned through my soul retrieval process when writing the *Realms of My Soul* poetry series that when we continue to ignore and sacrifice our own needs, patterns of self-neglect and judgement emerge, often accompanied by deep feelings of guilt and shame.

Unhealed childhood wounds often create an unrelenting cycle of suffering, where the pain of abandonment or betrayal embeds itself deep within our cellular body and mind.

These scars fuel the voice of our inner critic, keeping us trapped in a state of constant alert, convinced that we're never truly safe within ourselves. Stuck in survival mode, we turn this inner chaos outward, projecting our pain onto others through judgment and criticism.

The challenge is not only facing our past but recognizing how deeply ingrained patterns of people-pleasing continue to shape our everyday lives. Healing begins when we bring awareness to these hidden parts of ourselves, reconnecting with the inner child we abandoned in our pain.

As we soothe our nervous system and retrain our minds, we create space for new habits to form. Slowly, we reclaim trust and empathy, both for ourselves and for the world around us. This journey transforms how we view life, offering a path toward wholeness and self-compassion.

When I reflect back on the notion of "home", I realize that it wasn't a physical place—it was a feeling, a connection to something much larger than myself. I found solace in the night sky, imagining the stars as a sanctuary of total bliss. I would often ask, "What would love do in the cosmos?"

The answer was always the same: pure love would celebrate each star's light with harmony and acceptance. This sense of unity, of belonging, was something I carried within, even as I struggled with the disconnection that seemed to define life on Earth.

As I grew, I realized that every human being has an authentic essence, a unique expression within the nature of reality. Trauma and pain disconnect us from this essence, but healing brings us back to it.

This journey to rediscovering our true selves is a process of remembering who we are beyond the childhood wounding programs.

To make sense of the universe and my place in it, I turned to science, particularly quantum physics. I used my logical mind to explore the mysteries of existence, but it wasn't until my forties that I truly began to understand who I AM at my core.

As I immersed myself in quantum field theory, a new understanding of reality unfolded before me. This framework illuminated the profound interconnectedness of all things and the uncertainty that permeates existence, revealing the boundless potential lurking beneath the surface of our observable world.

In this paradigm, particles cease to be isolated entities; they transform into vibrations and ripples within a vast field. This shift in perspective uncovers the phenomenon of entanglement, where information can travel faster than light, highlighting the deep interrelation of the quantum field.

Rather than occupying fixed positions, particles exist as probabilities, their behaviors defined by wave functions that blur the boundaries between what is possible and what is certain.

I also discovered that the observer effect adds another layer of intrigue, suggesting that our very act of observation can influence the quantum field, prompting questions about the role of consciousness in shaping our reality.

Even the quantum vacuum, once considered empty, is teeming with potential energy and virtual particles, hinting at a sea of infinite possibilities.

This exploration led me to the tantalizing idea of parallel universes, each representing different outcomes of quantum events or timelines, expanding our perception of existence in ways we have yet to fully comprehend.

These perspectives dismantle conventional views, unlocking revolutionary ideas like multiple dimensions, the influence of consciousness, and the intricate energy interactions that shape every facet of our experience. In this realm, possibility is limitless, and the nature of reality is far more fluid than we ever thought possible.

From a Divine Design perspective, Source and the quantum field reveal profound principles of interconnectedness, unity, and limitless potential. Source embodies the fundamental essence of all creation, a singular force from which every being and event emerges, highlighting our deep connection through a divine web of energy.

Mirroring this, the quantum field thrives on dynamic energy, where particles vibrate and interact in a constant dance of possibilities. *This reflects Source as an ever-evolving force that generates and sustains life, emphasizing the flow of creativity throughout the universe.*

From my perspective, Source is viewed as the ultimate consciousness, with individuals embodying its divine awareness. This connection means our awareness influences our reality, just as thoughts and intentions can shape outcomes in the quantum realm.

Aligning with Source empowers us to manifest our highest potential, illustrating how our focus and energy can mold our experiences.

As the origin of all creation, Source gives rise to diverse expressions of life. Similarly, the quantum field encompasses infinite possibilities, celebrating the beauty of individuality within the collective whole.

Both Source and the quantum field exist beyond the constraints of time and space, functioning as timeless forces that profoundly influence and sustain the universe. In this grand tapestry, I have uncovered my connection to the Divine and recognized my ability to co-create reality within the boundless realm of Infinite Intelligence.

As an extension of the One Source, my consciousness plays a pivotal role in shaping my reality through intention and awareness. It influences the energy patterns that manifest in my physical form and experiences, revealing the power I hold to weave my destiny into the ever-unfolding fabric of universal existence.

So, by aligning our aspects of consciousness with the universal flow, we tap into higher states of awareness with our spiritual intelligence, accessing cosmic wisdom and our true potential as co-creators.

Our human body acts as an electromagnetic semiconductor, with our cells and chromosomes functioning like liquid crystals—fluid yet highly organized. This intelligent, crystalline structure runs through our DNA, nerve cells, connective tissue, and even the molecules in our muscles.

It's fascinating that these structures don't just conduct energy; *they also store it, amplify signals, and direct light throughout our bodies.*

Our connective tissue system processes solar light frequency and links every part of our biological system, while the brain and consciousness are quantum superconductors.

When we align the mind and the heart, we tap into our spiritual intelligence through this energetic gateway to higher frequencies.

This heart intelligence is the key to unlocking a deeper, more expansive state of awareness. With over 40,000 neurons, the heart is not just a pump but the body's main biological oscillator, setting the rhythms of our emotions and perceptions.

All of us have experienced being caught in a whirlwind of thoughts, fixating on something from our past—perhaps a memory from childhood. When we get triggered, like someone cutting in front of us on the road, it's often a reflection of stored emotional memories from earlier experiences.

Shifting into heart intelligence changes everything. Science shows that when we lead from the heart, we gain a new perspective, like zooming out to see the bigger picture.

Spiritually, as the heart awakens, so does our inner vision, the pineal gland, allowing us to perceive ourselves and others more clearly—not through the literal lens of the ego but with empathy and understanding.

Emotional intelligence, often overlooked in favor of IQ, plays a crucial role in our success. It correlates more with achievement in the workplace and material life.

As we initiate our heart's intelligence, we tap into a new way of perceiving and interacting with the world. We become more peaceful, creative, and unified, able to communicate clearly and forge deeper harmonious connections.

A *Coherent Heart* gives us the ability to slow down, respond thoughtfully, and avoid reactive behavior that blocks our potential for abundance and success. Living from the heart allows us to exist in a state of flow, where we are more connected to our true selves and the world around us, moment by moment.

For me, this interconnectedness explains how energy healing works and how our bodies store information at a molecular level. Understanding this has made me deeply aware of how the external information I absorb shapes my inner reality, making me more intentional about what I allow into my mind's awareness.

As Buddha stated, "The highest truth is that there is no beginning or end", emphasizing the idea that existence is an eternal principle of Natural Law, transcending the limitation of time. While time is finite, existence and consciousness are timeless.

If we exist, we are eternally One with Source, and this Gnosis unveils our essence as consciousness itself—self-aware intelligence interconnected with all that is and the I AM (Awareness Manifested).

From an esoteric perspective, Gnosis embodies a profound, intuitive knowledge that transcends intellectual comprehension, facilitating a direct experience of the spirit. This inner wisdom emerges from a deep connection to the unified field, a "knowing" often accessed through meditation and contemplation.

We embody universal consciousness in physical form, living out the eternal life force energy that connects us to all of existence.

While I don't usually use labels, I resonate deeply with this concept and the "Starseed" archetype. As a bearer of light, I feel an overwhelming cosmic connection that transcends the Earthly plane and the cycle of reincarnation.

There is a knowing within me—a deep-seated understanding—that my soul has origins in other dimensions or star systems, and that I volunteered to be here in this timeline with a specific mission.

I had a powerful moment of confirmation when I accidently encountered the teachings of Dolores Cannon in 2023, a hypnotherapist and past-life regressionist.

Her work on the waves of volunteers on Earth resonated deeply with my experiences. It felt as though her words were echoing what I had always known within myself, affirming my sense of purpose and connection to higher dimensions.

More and more people are opening up and sharing their stories as we move into this new earth frequency. Quantum physics has changed the way we perceive consciousness and energy, which is removing some of the stigma associated with real spiritual self-mastery.

It's inspiring to witness so many individuals embracing their truth, connecting with their higher-selves, and contributing to the collective awakening.

The shift towards a more conscious, loving, and unified existence is becoming palpable, and it's heartening to see others stepping into their light and connecting, just as I have.

This connection is not just a transient feeling; it's an intrinsic part of my being. It drives me to discern truth and seek wisdom from within, to understand my purpose here, to learn unity, to grow in love, and to expand my spiritual consciousness.

My journey is not only about my own growth, but about assisting in humanity's conscious evolution, as prophesized.

I recognize that we are more than just mind and body—*we are multidimensional beings, composed of stardust, crystalline semi-conductors, and spirit.* This intuitive awareness guides me on my path of sovereignty, embodying my true self as a Lightworker, an Alchemist, and an imperfect human on an individualized *Hero's Odyssey* to self-mastery.

To understand my soul's essence, I had to move beyond the confines of my logical mind, the survival-driven ego, and the boundaries of my physical identity. This journey required me to flow into the formless realms of consciousness, where my soul's multi-dimensional essence exists beyond the lower energetic fields of identity.

By choosing to unite with this flow state, guided by a higher creative Infinite Intelligence, I discovered a space where there are no boundaries, opposition, or resistance. Here, the soul simply is—an unmasked, naked representation of the fractal of Source, transcending the linearity of the ego's need to survive and prove its existence.

The ego, by nature, is rigid and driven by the necessity programs of the mind to protect, compete, and assert its specialness. This is often in contrast to the soul's desire to experience unity within the universal consciousness. However, *we cannot have this human experience without our ego—it's not our enemy to be killed or released.*

I realized that in the school of life, I had to partner up and integrate my survival-based ego by mastering its programs.

I sat in silence, faced my shadows through inner child healing, and re-engineered myself back to my core essence with inner work and self-realization. By aligning my mind with my *Heart's Coherence* and embracing the formless life force energy of my soul, I feel the beauty of Oneness and surrender.

In this academy, every choice and lesson unfolds in Divine order, guiding my growth and awakening. I understand that I only need to be aware of the options before me to choose the perspective I will use to experience them.

Each decision, even the ones that feel repetitive, has been intentionally placed before me, like pieces of my own customized curriculum. These moments are designed to help me grow, to encourage me to choose differently when the time is right. It's as if everything has already been scripted, and I am merely experiencing it all, moment by moment, as part of my soul's evolutionary story.

As I continue to observe a multidimensional movie of free will—the real question is: how am I watching it? Am I viewing it with my eyes open but my heart closed? Or am I embracing each moment with an open heart, knowing that even if I stumble, I am still elevating on my path to expansion?

The *perspective we choose* determines whether we feel like we are constantly failing or recognize the value in everything we have already achieved. *This realization is a reminder that growth and change are always happening, whether we see it clearly or not.*

Our consciousness can only expand as far as the limits of our caged belief system of our mind, often referred to as the matrix.

Now, as I embrace my *Hero's Odyssey* to self-mastery, my ego and soul's radiant life force energy walk together, hand in hand, harmonized in this ongoing process of self-discovery and path to enlightenment.

I believe that Earth is an *Ascending Angel Academy*—a physical school where our spirits come to learn, grow, expand, love unconditionally, and evolve. The tools and curriculum I have found helpful has been crafted in the philosophy of my soul.

Connecting Philosophy with Writing

In my creative work, I craft a vibrant tapestry of light and sacred geometry, drawing from the unified field of Source consciousness and the Akashic Records. This cosmic library contains the collective memories and experiences of every soul. It is an ethereal repository that allows us to access profound insights and wisdom, offering a deeper understanding of our purpose and interconnectedness within the universe.

I approach mystical concepts that resonate with my frequency by integrating the wisdom of masters that have walked before me—those spiritually enlightened beings who have transcended earthly reincarnation and achieved profound self-mastery.

While I don't channel entities like the Council of Light or the Galactic Federation, nor do I rely on ancient texts or Shamanism, I hold deep respect for the paths of traditional Yogis.

Instead, I blend insights from mystics and Ascended Masters such as Buddha, Krishna, Yeshua, Saint Germain, and Tesla, along with the principles of ancient Chinese medicine, all of which are intricately embedded in the archives of existence.

As these light codes flow through my auric field. I serve as a conduit, transcribing them into fictional books and poetic expressions. My storytelling skills help me interpret this information based on my current level of awareness and perception. I believe there's a fine line between imagination and reality.

Is it possible to create epic fantasy worlds, by tapping into an alternate universe, drawing from realms beyond our physical senses?

When we align with our higher selves, connected to the Divine Design, and tap into unseen dimensional realms, we each hold the power to access a vast wealth of universal information, unlocking the potential to co-create realities and generate magic.

Creative expression, love, and curiosity are the physical manifestations of the soul communicating with us through the higher self. Our soul transmits messages via energy, light codes, and frequency, and our bodies translate them into feelings of passion and excitement.

When something ignites within us, lights us up, it's our higher self delivering a spark of intuitive guidance, urging us to act. Do we listen to that whisper and nudge or ignore the call?

In the physical world, action is the language of commitment. By acting on what excites us, we tap into the unseen realms, creating a powerful exchange.

Our higher self continues to offer opportunities through passion, and each step we take signals our readiness to engage further with the universe, deepening that connection.

This flow state unlocks our creative force and synchronicity, pulling us deeper into alignment with our true path. Curiosity fuels growth, and joy becomes a natural byproduct. The more we act on these impulses, the more doors open, accelerating our journey toward purpose and fulfillment. It's a living dialogue with the universe, giving and receiving—each step we take strengthens the bond with our higher self and expands our potential.

This is the magnificent power of our human essence, which aligns the mind to the creative energy of the

Coherent Heart field—a precious gift that should never be compromised or jeopardized.

Writing and infusing my work with light code energy is my calling, purpose, and mission. Through this work, I aim to activate, empower, and inspire my reader's and their awakening journey as co-creators, contributing to human evolution through the art of literature.

All of my published books include metaphysical views, lived experiences, life lessons, and perspectives. I incorporate esoteric wisdom, alchemy, hermetic principles, Gnosis, universal laws, and ancient cosmic insight into this philosophy—concepts that resonate deeply with my inner knowing.

When writing my poetry books, specifically the *Realms of My Soul* series, I often explore the delicate balance between personal growth and the actuality of relationships with our light body, with spirit, mind, heart, nature, and within the universe.

But first, I had to trek through the fiery remembrance and rapture of my innocence.

I embarked on my soul retrieval where I found her—my inner child, just three years old, with her shaved head and wide, curious eyes. She was waiting for me, frozen in time, longing to be seen, to be whole again.

This was a part of me I had forgotten, the purest version of myself—brimming with imagination, life force resilience, and the limitless dreams of a child. But somewhere along the way, that light had faded, and I had lost her.

As I journeyed back through the *Realms of My Soul*, I realized how much I had let the world silence me. Every wound, every harsh judgment twisted my essence, contorting me into something I no longer recognized.

Little by little, I fractured—lost in the noise of other people's expectations, believing that my worth was something I had to earn with people-pleasing behaviors to feel safe. The more I tried to fit into this world, the more I abandoned her, that little girl inside who just wanted to be free and to be seen.

I reflected on how deeply I had betrayed myself in survival mode, how I gave away my power piece by piece, believing that love meant sacrifice, that my value was tied to the approval of others.

I became trapped in the patterns of codependency, wrapped in the chains of pleasing others, desperately seeking validation. The world mirrored back my wounds, and I believed those narratives as my truth.

But in the darkest corners of my soul, I found the courage to face the pain. I descended into the void, into the depths of my shadow, where trauma blocked my rays of light.

It was there, in the emptiness, that I found myself again—not in the external world, but deep within the layers of my being. I embraced the hurt, the loneliness, the raw agony of feeling forgotten, and in that darkness, I began to rise.

This was my resurrection, the moment when I began piecing myself back together, uniting fragment by fragment, memory by memory. It was a spiral of remembering, a sacred journey of reclaiming the parts of me that had been frozen in time.

With every step, I moved closer to wholeness, further along this *Hero's Odyssey*—a path that has crumbled me, healed me, and transformed me in ways I never imagined. Soul retrieval was a challenging journey, but its beauty lay in reconnecting me with the innocence I thought was lost forever. It restored the very essence of who I am.

Capturing these feelings in my poetry is more than just an artistic expression; they are deeply rooted in my personal philosophy, which bridge the ethereal aspects of metaphysics with practical, earthly human experiences, offering insights that can be applied to everyday life.

Part 1 of this book is intended to offer my viewpoints, combining philosophy and reflections to help you connect with your divine essence. This is done by acknowledging the interrelation of all things, finding ways to nurture self-love and fostering personal growth with grace.

However, with the chaos and turmoil of the external world, this isn't just a philosophical discourse; it's a call to action.

My intention is to inform you how these esoteric concepts, often explored in abstract terms, can actually enhance your daily life, to go from an inflamed nervous system in survival mode to an aligned, balanced and peaceful way of being.

It is for anyone seeking growth, healing, awareness, or a deeper sense of purpose, guiding you on an interdimensional journey of mind, heart, body, and spirit.

Along this path, you have the choice of taking back your power, activating your spiritual intelligence with inner peace as alchemists and mystics, changing your lives from within.

In Part 2, the poetry explores deeper themes such as understanding the pain body, navigating life's transitions and uncomfortable change, self-discovery, recognizing essential relationships, and achieving self-actualization with mastery. These poems are infused with the philosophy of my soul, a practice of embodiment.

I invite you to journey with me beyond the verses of poetry into the realm of metaphysics, "a fundamental nature of knowledge, reality, and the interconnectedness of existence, consciousness, and energy".

Together, we will delve into the deeper layers of perspectives that shape our understanding of the world and ourselves. Whether it's through the practice of mindfulness, the cultivation of inner peace with radical self-love and inner-work, or the deepening of your spiritual awareness, the goal is to empower you to free your mind from negatively charged, polarized thought forms.

My hope is that as you read, you will gain a profound understanding of the concepts that inspire my work, while also discovering practical ways to apply them in your own life. The experiences and lessons captured in the narrative sonnets that follow in Part 2 are meant to act as a catalyst and guide on your path toward deeper self-awareness.

This path begins by embracing and nurturing the vulnerable aspects of our humanity, acknowledging the patterns of childhood wounding without bypassing the unresolved pain or trauma we carry in our bodies.

These blockages in our energy fields must be addressed to fully feel, heal, and expand.

When we open our heart field and live authentically, without masks or filters, we create the possibility of experiencing a unified world filled with compassion, safety, peace, and harmony. This allows us to release the struggle and suffering patterns that often burden our lives.

Ultimately, as co-creators, we are each responsible for our own reactions, thoughts, feelings, and actions. By embracing this authority, we reclaim our personal power and sovereignty.

Our souls have incarnated in this individualized simulation of reality as expressions of Divine Source energy, ultimately destined to reunite within the Logos of Oneness. This Divine principle encompasses order, reason, and creative expression, serving as the foundational essence from which all creation emerges.

However, within this journey, *our human emotions and the suffering experienced on Earth are undeniably real and significant.*

We can transcend our individual suffering story by allowing every emotion to be our guide and teacher—feeling deeply and exploring the insights and redirection each inner sensation reveals.

In these depths, we uncover understanding, wisdom, and clarity, discovering the essential lessons needed for growth and awakening.

Once we balance the lower three energy fields of ego survival-based programs within our biofield, we open our heart center with empathy. This is when we activate our free will and align with Divine Will to help ascend and uplevel to the next event of conscious expansion.

The purest form of unbounded love is to be in service to others, either by showing up each day with an open heart, sharing a kind smile with a stranger, having the courage to tell your unique story to inspire another or advocating for the innocence of every child, nature, and being to assist in the evolution of our planet.

When we integrate the shadow aspects of ourselves, our collective light grows stronger, illuminating the path forward. Each step we take transforms that darkness into a source of strength, fueling the brilliance that rests within.
This journey is a powerful reminder that you are already a radiant spark, a magnificent gift of pure essence, destined to shine and thrive.

May these words guide you in embracing every part of yourself, just as they are, until only devotion remains—no matter the unexpected emotions that may arise. In freedom of acceptance, no matter how life ebbs and flows, may you always remember that you are loved, exactly as you are.

Thank you for taking the time to explore your *Coherent Heart*, to align with the power of your higher-self, and to embrace your *Hero's Odyssey* to self-mastery as you navigate the tides of change.

As always, please take what resonates with your spirit and nourishes your soul. I honor your Divine essence and your gift of light.

Fundamental Concepts

At the core of my understanding rests the belief that pure love is the essence of our being and the highest objective truth of the universe, guided by the laws of balance and harmony.

This love is not just an emotion; it is who we are, the fundamental force without bounds that connects us with all existence, the unifying thread that binds everything in the cosmos.

This "Source" of pure love consciousness is known by many names; the unified quantum field, Oneness, primordial Divinity, Supreme Infinite Intelligence, the God particle, the One Creator, Divine eternal being, omnipresence, and "The All".

From my perspective, when removing the religious lens of dogma, "Divinity" can be seen as the ability to transcend our perceived human limitations. It represents the essence of our life force, not to just survive but to triumph in this reality.

The path often requires reaching a state of elevated awareness that goes beyond ordinary experience, allowing us to fully embrace the richness and depth of existence.

Every individual possesses the power to recognize or reject the reality of our divine nature. We can choose to embrace the perception that we are all interconnected expressions of the Divine, or we can deny this fundamental reality, separating from Source.

This interpretation views Divinity as an inherent quality within all beings or existence, emphasizing the idea of wholeness and an inner connection to a higher state of consciousness or universal truth. It shifts the focus from external deities to the internal, expansive potential present in every individual and the universe itself.

Divinity embodies qualities such as purity, wisdom, compassion, and the expansive consciousness of love. It signifies the spiritual essence that goes beyond physical existence, linking all creation to a higher purpose or Infinite Intelligence. This divine energy pervades everything, guiding us toward deeper understanding and connection.

Understanding Consciousness:

In my view, conflict often arises from a deeper philosophical misunderstanding of existence. At its heart, this disconnect comes from our tendency to view consciousness and existence as separate, as if they are distinct forces at play. By isolating what happens in our minds from the world around us, we fracture our thoughts, words, and actions, leading to confusion and inner discord.

However, consciousness and existence are inseparable. Our external reality is not apart from us; it's an indivisible reflection of our own consciousness and essence. The awareness of our mind is intimately woven into the same consciousness that shapes existence itself. This unity may appear fragmented, but it divides only to experience the infinite layers of reality.

Together, this interconnectedness forms the very essence of who we are—our soul. Consciousness and existence are one and the same, interwoven into the fabric of all that is, inseparable from our being.

What makes us unique, however, is the lens through which we interpret this reality, processing our emotions and experiences based on our beliefs. Recognizing our emotions as sacred gifts allows us to perceive life with wonder and gratitude. These feelings, in all their complexity, are central to our human experience, anchoring us to the essence of being alive and driving our evolution.

By embracing the depth of our emotions, we transform ordinary moments into profound experiences. Each feeling becomes a conduit to the Divine, enriching our connection to life and fostering grace and appreciation throughout our journey. It's through this emotional depth that we engage with the beauty of our world, fully savoring the richness of existence.

In Esoteric wisdom, the Hermetics believed that all of existence occurs within the one cosmic mind of THE ALL, the infinite and omnipresent Source. They viewed the material universe—comprising energy, matter, and life—as existing at a lower vibration or at a slower wavelength than spirit.

The principles governing the higher plane of consciousness are reflected in those that direct the lower plane of matter, suggesting a fundamental unity between the two realms. *As above, so below.*

There is also a scientific theory that's been published, combining quantum physics and neuroscience. It suggests that our minds may exist in another dimension, similar to a black hole, with consciousness potentially operating independently of the brain.

The peer-reviewed scientific journal **NeuroQuantology** explores how quantum phenomena like entanglement and tunneling could explain rapid subconscious processes and shed light on the mind-brain connection.

I have come to realize that the mind processes information far faster than the current understanding of neural transmissions implies, suggesting that consciousness extends beyond mere brain activity. This perspective reveals a more expansive view, one that connects us to something far greater.

In this view, consciousness isn't confined to the physical body but acts as a bridge between our individual reality and the vast, interconnected universe. It links us to an immense, interstellar network—perhaps resembling a torus field, where energy flows endlessly in and out.

This network isn't just theoretical; it's alive, intelligent, constantly processing and organizing information in a holographic realm beyond what we normally perceive.

This theory delves even deeper, proposing that our thoughts and mental experiences may extend into additional spatial dimensions, far beyond the familiar boundaries of time and space. In this expanded dimension, our inner world is intricately woven into the very framework of the universe.

At the heart of this connection is our DNA, present in every cell of our body, acting as a powerful antenna. It is continuously receiving and transmitting signals across an expansive spectrum, engaging in a dynamic exchange with the universe. This process is far from passive—it's an active, ongoing conversation between our essence and the cosmic forces that shape our reality.

Each of our fifty trillion cells, composed of trillions of atoms, is in continuous interaction with the unified quantum field. In an eternal dance, these cells emerge from and return to this field, a dynamic exchange of energy and information. This constant interplay reflects the profound connection between our physical bodies and the unseen forces of the universe, illustrating how every part of us is interconnected to existence.

Even more astonishing is how our atoms respond to our consciousness. They are not fixed or permanent; *they shift and reorganize based on the energy we project.*

When we alter our beliefs or perspectives, we shift our awareness. The very building blocks of our physical form reshape themselves and transform. This is the essence of extraordinary healing—it is not some unattainable phenomenon, but the direct result of how we align with universal energy.

As our consciousness shifts, so too do the atoms within us, reshaping to fill the new template of our being. This transformation reflects the fluid relationship between our inner awareness and the physical world, where the changes in our consciousness guide the very structure of our existence. Every thought, intention, and realization reconfigures the atoms, aligning our physical self with the evolving essence of our remembrance.

For far too long, we have been conditioned to see ourselves as fragile, flawed beings, dependent on external forces to "fix" us. But the latest revelations from science tell a different story: *We are powerful, adaptable, and capable of extraordinary transformation through the consciousness we hold.*

Our ability to shift our awareness enables us to shape our reality, continuously evolving and transcending limitations. This inherent power allows us to reimagine ourselves, adapt to new circumstances, and transform our lives in profound ways, guided by the limitless potential of our consciousness.

This shift in mindset reveals that we are not merely victims of our biology but the co-creators of our reality. By tapping into the unified quantum field, we can actively shape our lives and experiences.

Our potential is boundless, and the key to unlocking it resides in our self-awareness. Embracing this understanding empowers us to transcend limitations and establish the experience we desire.

I have come to realize that one of our most profound missions is to honor and nurture the human vessel that allows us to express our Divinity in the world.
This requires the courage to rewire our minds, transforming our thought patterns and reshape how we relate to our bodies, the Earth, and the Cosmos. By embracing the unified quantum field with devotion, we anchor our highest potential and live authentically.

When we recognize that we are all connected through this unified consciousness, it becomes clear that chasing material fulfillment or seeking external validation and salvation stems from a false perception of lack. In truth, we are already whole. Understanding our interconnectedness with everything around us dissolves the illusion of emptiness or separation.

This divine, universal consciousness is as infinite as the love we hold for our children, our Earth, and the innocent animals that grace our lives. It is a love that transcends all boundaries—free from fear, bias, judgment, or conditions. It is pure, radiant, and ever-present, connecting us to the very essence of existence.

Pure love, by its very nature, can never cause harm—whether through our words, thoughts, or actions. Why would we choose to hurt another when each being reflects our own divinity, a mirror of our essence, or the innocent child that lives within every human?

The principle of "do no harm" is deeply rooted in biblical teachings, emphasizing devotion, kindness, and empathy. Verses like Romans 13:10 and Matthew 7:12 remind us that true love refrains from causing injury and fulfills the law by treating others as we wish to be treated.

Natural Law, Dharma, or Cosmic Law is also ancient wisdom that governs the moral foundation of Earth's dense reality. It operates on a simple but profound code: Do no harm, but also take no crap.

This understanding calls for balance—compassion and integrity must guide our actions, but we cannot allow ourselves to be passive or complacent in the face of polarization.

In this dense realm, where the illusion of separation can tempt us to either apathy or conflict, Cosmic Law reminds us of our active role in shaping our collective environment.

We cannot simply stand by and let external forces dictate the moral landscape. Instead, we have to be fully engaged in the pursuit of justice, freedom for all, and balance, consciously choosing actions that align with our moral compass.

I have realized that sometimes, it is not enough to be observers; we are co-creators of our communal reality, and our choices matter. By taking gentle non-violent action with wisdom and pure love, we contribute to the evolution of our collective consciousness, maintaining harmony within ourselves and the world around us.

In esoteric terms, this pure love is often symbolized by the archetype of Christ consciousness, representing the perfect state of spiritual being. It is a ray of light that connects all forms to Source energy, the unified quantum field of Oneness, or the God particle. It symbolizes the realization that all forms, whether light or dark, is an extension of Source.

This state of Christ consciousness, which emanates from the Greek word Christos, means "the Anointed One". It is within us all as we become aware of the eternal bond that links all beings, transcending separation and duality.

It is the realization that we are not only connected to Source but are the physical manifestations within human experience. We are active participants in Divine's ongoing creation through a mystical truth that can be felt and experienced in both the light and dark times of life.

Observing these insights reveals the core qualities of love, devotion, courage, and surrender, embodying these virtues in our own lives. Many people are aligned with this archetype or teachings because it's associated with the concepts of "fire" or "light."

When I removed myself from the dualistic doctrine and dogma, I finally understood the real meaning of this archetype as *a state of unity and enlightened awareness that transcends the material world, existing in realms of non-dual light.* I simply know it as pure love consciousness.

It represents a profound sense of Oneness with all existence, free from polarized illusions, where one aligns with inner wisdom and universal knowledge, recognizing the inherent unity within all life.

No matter what labels or language we use to articulate the ascension process, all signs of our human evolution are pointing to the epoch of unity consciousness.

This golden age of embodiment requires us to recognize that we are both unique, individualized expressions of Divine and, simultaneously, the Whole within Source itself.

Realizing our Spirit

We are souls experiencing life in human form, yet our true essence resides in spirit, an eternal realm where we always exist. From a metaphysical perspective, we never truly leave this spiritual dimension; physical reality is merely a dream woven into our soul's journey. Our soul continually guides the mind and body, ensuring our connection to spirit remains intact.

Spirit is a fundamental aspect of reality, transcending multiple dimensions and planes of existence. *It is the core energy that animates all living beings and unites everything in the universe*, omnipresent through creation while preserving the harmony of all life.

Described as infinite, formless, and boundless, spirit embodies pure essence and awareness. It fuels evolution, growth, and the expansion of consciousness, guiding us toward self-realization and a profound sense of oneness with the cosmos. Operating through universal laws like the Law of Vibration and the Law of Attraction, spirit shapes our experiences according to the frequencies we emit.

As a source of intuition, creativity, and higher wisdom, spirit serves as a bridge between physical and metaphysical realms, unlocking pathways to deeper truths about our existence. This connection enables us to cultivate a greater sense of inner peace and purpose through practices such as meditative contemplation and mindfulness.

Ultimately, spirit is the eternal essence within us, transcending the limitations of physical life and harmonizing with the infinite intelligence of the universe. Through our bond with spirit, we uncover the true nature of reality and our role in the grand, interconnected web of existence.

The temporary forgetting of our divine nature at birth allows us to explore life from new perspectives, rediscovering ourselves with each experience. In this journey of self-discovery, creation itself expands, evolving with every encounter, relationship, and eternal connections.

The Role of the Heart

The heart center plays a vital role in receiving messages from our spirit, acting as a bridge between the higher self and the brain. It captures direct vibrations from the soul, while the brain processes this information through its belief systems.

When we release fear-based or negative beliefs, our physical mind can better align with the wisdom of the heart, allowing us to function as a unified whole.

In this harmony, the heart beats in sync with the soul's guidance, while the brain, designed to navigate the present moment, is not meant to control everything. Instead, it helps us traverse physical reality, while the higher self provides insights into what lies ahead.

When heart, mind, body, and spirit are aligned, we move through life with greater cohesion, embracing creativity and ease.

Activating the Radio Antenna

These principles have guided my awakening, sparked by the activation of my third eye known as the pineal gland. This path has encompassed healing childhood wounds, uncovered trauma patterns, and engaging in somatic emotional wellbeing.

Along the way, I have delved into light work, shadow integration, crystalline grid healing, soul retrieval, organic medicine, and the *transformative arts of mastery, alchemy, and embodiment.*

All of these concepts have provided me with the tools needed on my path to restoration and self-discovery. The ongoing exploration of various modalities were brought into my awareness organically and continues to help me achieve a profound sense of harmony and self-love as I navigate my *Hero's Odyssey* in this lifetime.

Foundations of Alchemy

Alchemy is the ancient art of purification and transformation, both of matter and the self. At its core, alchemy seeks to strip away impurities, reducing a substance to its most refined essence—whether it's metal to gold or the human psyche.

This process of transmutation reveals our ultimate potential. We can alchemize a negative charge through transmutation, the act of evolving a base dense form into a higher frequence state. It is not just a physical transformation but a spiritual one.

In Esoteric terms, it is used as a metaphor for personal evolution, where alchemy guides us through stages of growth, from lead—representing ignorance or limitation—to gold, symbolizing enlightenment. Transmutation, in essence, is spiritual evolution, a process that mirrors the shifts of consciousness.

The deepest mystery of alchemy is its role in liberating the soul from the illusion of separation. It is the process by which the Divine Source stimulates its creation to rescue fragments of its soul that have become trapped in the dream of material density. This journey of return is an act of salvation, where Divine awakens itself from the illusion, returning to unity.

Cristos, or the illuminated state of being, remains untouched by the fall of mankind or corruption. The process of alchemy—transmutation, regeneration, and creation—has always existed as a fundamental structure of reality.

The symbolic nature of alchemy, including the Philosopher's Stone and the fifth element, represents this transformation from base to solar consciousness, which is also known as enlightenment.

At the heart of alchemy is the fifth element, which the ancients referred to as the primal force of creation—also known as *spirit*, ether, primal light, and sound.

This essence holds the blueprint of the universe, containing the potential for everything that exists within the Akashic Records.

Our spirit is the force that organizes thoughts, emotions, and intentions, explaining why our thoughts create our physical reality. By interacting with this primal essence, we can direct and shape it, influencing outcomes in the material world.

As I understand it, the art of alchemy operates uniquely for each individual, responding to the chemistry of our awareness. Ultimately, it is a Divine salvation, unifying the mind and *Coherent Heart*, and initiating us into higher states of being.

It is how we begin our *Hero's Odyssey*, our spiritual activation and awakening, guiding us toward our highest potential of Cosmic Law—transforming us from within to embody our true nature.

In 2016, I experienced an intuitive calling to share these foundational concepts from my perspective with the art of storytelling. And so, I published my first metaphysical thriller, *Heart of a Warrior Angel: From Darkness to Light* in 2019.

This fictional book revolves around themes of transformation, overcoming tragedy, self-actualization, the power of forgiveness, and empowerment, featuring characters who confront their childhood wounds, and fight shadows with their eternal light force energy.

I continued to blend my philosophy with science fiction fantasy in *The De-Coding of Jo* series, delving into the fundamental nature of reality, existence, and the co-creation of harmonious truths.

In these stories, the protagonists use metaphysics and energy transmutation to transform shadows into light, guided by the Solfeggio harmonic frequency, self-love, vulnerability, compassion, and acceptance.

When the world shut down in 2020, I asked the Universe a genuine, heartfelt question: how may I be in service for the highest good? The answers poured through my radio antenna known as the pineal gland to unseen dimensions in waves of golden hues and crystalline frequency.

I experienced an elevated state of awareness, entering into a meditative service of prayer for our precious world. I reached this blissful state naturally, without the aid of plant medicine or psychedelics.

I had the privilege and honor of uniting and collaborating with other intuitive artists to publish *The Joy of I.T. (Infinite Transcendence).*

This coffee table book is infused with healing light codes and unifying love frequencies, featuring transformational poetry and full-color artwork that are meant to uplift and delight the senses.
Our intention was to spread joy and magic through a challenging and dark period on the planet, by focusing our attention within our hearts where gratitude lives.

During this time, however, I became aware of my detachment from human emotions. This awareness highlighted the importance of truly feeling and recognizing the powerful, transformative messages embedded within our emotional intelligence as part of human experience.

However, escaping to the blissful realms defied my mission of being present at every moment.

The Catalyst

When I was crafting *The De-Coding of Jo* series, I had a profound realization about my soul's evolution. I imagined myself graduating from Earth's third density as if I was attending a school for celestial beings, an *Angel Academy*. I knew that balancing my energy centers mirrored the divine harmony of Source.

The Divine split its golden light or Logos, into seven distinct colors in our biofield, also known as chakras or the color wheel of rays. Each of us embodies these hues in our auric field in unique ways.

As we elevate our energy to the indigo ray—the third eye—we unlock the gateway to Infinite Intelligence, touching the singularity of Source, love consciousness.

Initially, I worried about activating my powerful gifts, however, I have learned that the true focus was not on the stimulation of abilities but on understanding the catalysts—experiences that initiate and elevate our energy centers. These catalysts are essential for raising our consciousness and spiritual intelligence.

I have found that a catalyst is any experience, often negatively charged, that sparks our seven energy centers and drives growth.

A trigger occurs when this experience causes a moment of nervous system dysregulation.

When a catalyst enters our life, it first impacts the red ray, or root field, located at the base of the vertebrae. This is where the journey of light begins, passing through our spinal network like a filtration system for cosmic energy as it ascends.

Childhood trauma shapes our identity, often leaving us with deep feelings of brokenness, unworthiness, or shame. These unhealed wounds manifest in the stories we tell ourselves, feeding the intrusive thoughts we mistake for truth.

Distress lingers in the body, creating an energetic imprint that traps us in a constant state of alertness. Trauma isn't just emotional or mental—it settles into our fascia, the connective tissue that encases every bone, nerve, and organ. In response to stress, fascia tightens and thickens, causing tension that echoes long after the event has passed.

Without processing, this tension can lead to chronic pain or autoimmune conditions, locking the nervous system in a cycle of hypervigilance that makes us feel unsafe in our own bodies. Healing requires reconnection—through mindful meditative movement, slow breathwork, and somatic release exercises.

Activating the parasympathetic nervous system is essential. Techniques like vagus nerve stimulation, cold exposure, or even singing can help release stored trauma, restoring a sense of safety and freedom within.

It is important to understand that the root field governs our primal needs and survival instincts in Earth's third density, where the belief in lack begins.
This deep-rooted fear of survival stems from an ancient place in our brain, perceiving any unmet need—whether for food, shelter, or companionship—as a potential threat.

When the root field is unbalanced, catalytic energy struggles to rise, trapping us in a cycle of fight-or-flight, where every experience is filtered through the lens of survival.

Recognizing this, I started to confront my core fears, healing my inner child and retrieving lost aspects of my soul.
By doing so, I balanced my root ray and unlocked the full potential of my catalytic experiences, propelling me further on my journey of consciousness expansion.

I have learned that unresolved pain doesn't just affect our bodies; it seeps into relationships, trust, self-worth, and self-care. The stress of suppressed trauma can send cortisol levels soaring. In response, calmness and inner peace have become my self-love language, a path to balance and healing.

It is remarkable how often people respond with hostility when their rigid beliefs or external narratives are challenged. These reactions usually signal a blocked root field, keeping energy stuck and preventing it from rising to higher centers. This leaves them in a constant state of survival mode, where anger masks deeper emotions.

I have come to understand that anger is often a shield for the vulnerability of sadness, frustration, rejection, humiliation, or loneliness.
When anger rises, I now ask myself: "What basic need isn't being met right now?" This question has helped me process those emotions in a healthy way, integrating and balancing my energetic fields.

I also welcomed isolation and loneliness into my heart like an old friend, treating them with the same respect as any other part of me. Each time these feelings overwhelmed me, I acknowledged them, grateful for their trust in sharing doubts, regrets, and embarrassment.

Even when I was feeling burdened by this emotion, I provided it with safe space, being a faithful listener and companion. I gave myself permission to embrace these emotions as valued parts of my life, even when I longed for different circumstances.

With this approach, the guarded door to my heart slowly opened, unblocking pain and hurt to transform into an empowered state and the highest frequency—unconditional love and devotion.

In the third density or physical world, the fight-or-flight response is essential for human survival, triggered by the sympathetic nervous system when danger looms. It readies the body to either face the threat or flee, flooding us with adrenaline, raising our heart rate, and sharpening our focus.

This response is vital for immediate action in life-threatening situations, but it's meant to be temporary. When the body remains in this heightened state for too long, as with chronic stress, it can lead to severe physical and emotional imbalances.

Far too many are suffering in a prolonged disempowered state of stress in today's society.
I recognize that mental health challenges and emotional exhaustion are very real, and I have personally felt and lived with their heavy burden.

Having struggled with anxiety, depression, and multiple burnouts, I have experienced the profound effects of an overwhelmed nervous system trapped in a state of freeze.

Addressing the mental health crisis is vital for breaking down the stigma and shame that so often accompany these struggles. This mission is at the heart of my writing and storytelling, reflecting my deep commitment to advocating for self-love and healing through the *Realms of My Soul.*

By delving into these issues openly, I strive to raise awareness, nurture empathy, and encourage a more supportive dialogue around mental health. To shift perceptions, we must take a proactive and compassionate approach. It is essential to emphasize that mental health challenges are not a reflection of personal weakness but rather a shared human experience.

Openly sharing personal stories can bridge gaps in understanding, illustrating that these struggles are part of our collective journey. By fostering safe spaces for open conversations in our communities, workplaces, and schools, we can dispel myths and create a culture where mental health is addressed with genuine respect and care.

This effort helps build a supportive environment and vital relationships where every individual feels seen, heard, and understood.

Through my journey, I have discovered the profound impact of open and conscious communication in relationships. Embracing vulnerability and valuing honest dialogue, rather than retreating into defensiveness, is crucial for building genuine connections and fostering healing.

This approach not only deepens relationships but also creates an environment where both understanding and growth can flourish.

Meeting our Human Needs

As humans, we possess several primary needs that are essential for our physical, emotional, and psychological well-being. These needs can be broadly categorized into physiological, safety, social, esteem, and self-actualization.

At the foundation of human existence rests our physiological needs, which are essential for survival and well-being. Food and water provide the energy and nutrients we need to function, while shelter offers protection from the elements and a safe space to rest.

Sleep is crucial for physical and mental health, allowing our bodies and minds to rejuvenate. Additionally, clothing protects us from environmental factors and reflects our personal identity.

Access to healthcare and wellness resources ensures that we maintain our health, allowing us to thrive rather than merely survive.

Beyond these physiological essentials, our safety needs play a vital role in fostering a secure and stable life. A safe living environment, free from threats or violence, is fundamental for peace of mind.

Financial security and reliable employment create a stable foundation, enabling us to focus on personal growth without constant worry. Furthermore, health security, which includes access to healthcare, protects us against illness and supports our overall well-being.

Recognizing our fundamental needs is essential for understanding the key factors that contribute to emotional well-being. By fulfilling these needs, particularly for our inner child, we open the door to a balanced and enriching life, allowing us to thrive personally and socially.

In my journey, I have come to realize that every individual has basic emotional needs that must be regulated on the path to healing. Neglecting these needs can lead to feelings of anxiety, depression, and isolation, stripping us of the peace and connection we truly seek.

Therefore, it is crucial to become aware of our emotional regulation patterns, as they guide us toward self-awareness and growth, ultimately empowering us to embrace a more fulfilling life:

Belonging: One of the most profound needs I have learned to address is to feel that *I belong* in this world. For me, this sense of feeling valued stems from understanding my purpose and meaning in life.
The need to feel connected to others, whether through family, animals, friendships, or community also offers a sense of acceptance. It can also include pursuing a creative passion, building a career, or finding a

supportive tribe. Knowing why I exist gives me a sense of rootedness and reason for living, understanding the role I play in contributing to the evolution of humanity.

Safety: Another vital need is feeling secure in my body, especially for my inner child. This sense of safety comes from living in an environment where I can be my authentic self without needing to defend, justify, or hide. When my body feels safe, I can relax in a parasympathetic state, allowing genuine connections with myself and others.

This is the space where I am able to let my guard down, not walk on eggshells, and truly feel free. Fulfilling the need for a stable environment is crucial for children to safely express emotions without fear of judgment or retribution. It encourages openness and vulnerability.

Autonomy: Regaining my sense of independence has been a major part of my healing. I have reclaimed my power, especially in overcoming co-dependent behaviors. Realizing that I have a voice, that I can make choices about my values, feelings, relationships, and boundaries, has given me confidence and self-trust.

When a major catalyst activated my throat field, I began to express my needs, healthy boundaries, and my heart's desires with clarity and resolve. Fulfilling the need for personal agency and the ability to make choices are vital for emotional well-being.

Vital Relationships: During my time living alone, I realized how deeply I longed for physical connection and intimacy. As humans, we thrive on social bonds, and having someone who understands us without judgment—someone who truly listens and values our presence—is essential to feeling balanced and whole. When I can connect through touch, hugs and eye contact, I feel seen and accepted for who I am, not for what I can do for others.

Challenge and Growth: I have come to view every challenge or trigger as an opportunity for growth. These moments, though difficult, push me to resolve underlying issues, learn, and trust in my ability to overcome adversity. This journey has made me more resilient and confident, elevating with strength along the way while I navigate emotional releases. Fulfilling this need helps me to process and heal from past hurts. Forgiveness, both for myself and others, allows for emotional freedom with the ability to grow and move forward.

Self-Awareness: The most difficult task on our journey of growth is to connect with our true self, the pure soul that incarnated in this physical realm, also known as the inner child. This means that we have to be aware of our behaviors, thoughts, feelings, and reactions to transform. Self-soothing and calming my nervous system after stressful situations are critical skills I have developed.

It took time and perseverance, but I learned how to regulate my emotions when I feel misunderstood, especially in a world dominated by disempowering media narratives. Pursuing personal development fosters resilience and a sense of achievement fulfilling the need to evolve.

Decompression: In today's fast-paced, highly connected world of social media, I have discovered the importance of decompression. My nervous system often feels overwhelmed, and without moments to quiet my mind and reconnect through meditation or mindfulness, it's difficult to find balance. Taking the time to decompress from the external noise and chaos helps me restore my energy and re-center.

When we actively address and nurture these primary needs, we cultivate a profound sense of fulfillment and connection, enhancing our quality of life and fostering healthier communities. Each need plays a critical role in shaping our experiences and interactions, influencing our relationships, choices, and sense of purpose in the world.

Together, these needs form the bedrock of a balanced, energetically coherent life of authenticity and vulnerability. It unifies us with relatable experiences and empowers us to create a positively charged reality with meaningful connections, to pursue our aspirations with confidence.

Through all of this, I have learned that boundaries, emotional intelligence, and honest self-reflection are key to healing and transformation. We are here to grow, feel, and be real with ourselves.

Our emotions serve as gateways to deeper self-awareness, guiding us toward the lessons we need to confront and understand. By embracing our feelings, we unlock the potential for profound growth, propelling ourselves toward a higher, more aligned path in life. It is through this emotional acceptance that we transcend our limitations and step into a new realm of possibilities.

We also have a duty to pass on emotional resilience and morality to the next generation. To be soft and to feel are not a sign of weakness. In fact, resilience rises from the courage to embrace our vulnerabilities, where true strength lies not in perfection, but in the raw, unguarded moments we often try to hide.

When we face our deepest challenges head-on, with all our fears and uncertainties laid bare, we discover the unshakable power within us to rise, heal, and transcend. By confronting our trials with openness, we cultivate the inner fortitude to grow and persevere.

Our children deserve to grow up witnessing respect, healthy conflict resolution, conscious communication, and mutual support.

No amount of financial wealth can replace the values of empathy, compassion, kindness, integrity, and self-respect. It's up to us to create homes where these qualities thrive.

On my healing journey, I have also become aware of the toxic patterns that once dictated my life. I used to believe I had to fix everything and everyone as I navigated survival mode. In adulthood, this belief led to burnout, emotional exhaustion, and feeling taken advantage of or used.

I broke free from this narrative by cutting energetic cords and setting boundaries, knowing I'm not responsible for other people's emotions, decisions, or spiritual well-being.

While this approach may disappoint loved ones, I had to stop enabling those stuck in a victimhood mentality. I realized that healing required me to protect my own energetic fields, to fill my cup first before helping others.

Prioritizing my physical, emotional, and spiritual well-being has become an essential practice in my daily life. The harsh truth is that anyone who tries to guilt, shame, or condemn us is projecting their own issues and disrespecting our boundaries.
So, we hold space for them from afar, without judgement while they confront their lessons of transcendence.

Healthy relationships are built on reciprocal connection—where both parties' needs are met, and the dynamic is not chronically exhausting.

It is also very natural to have dysregulated emotions, they are part of life, signaling that our body is processing something important.

When someone disrespects us, violates our boundary, or betrays us, it is a sign that we are connected to the emotional experience of heartbreak or loss. This can look like sadness, rage, or feeling indifferent. No human being is meant to be calm or stagnant all the time.

Emotions bring us messages that we need to process to clear the blockages in our auric field. Dysregulation is actually emotional energy that needs to be moved through the body's seven energy centers via a physical outlet.

Punching a bag, screaming into a pillow, going for a long walk, or watching a sad movie while sobbing into a towel helps us release physical energy and return to a parasympathetic state.

I have learned the hard way, through toxic positivity, that denying our emotions or pressuring ourselves to pretend to feel positive is just another form of suppression.

Our bodies need to feel and be released on a regular basis.

Having the ability to regulate our emotions means that we can express our feelings in a healthy way then recover from them. It's a sign that we are not on autopilot, numbing ourselves, or in a state of freeze.

It is important to recognize that those who seem to have everything together all the time may actually be navigating a dissociative state, where they struggle to feel anything at all. Beneath their composed exterior could lie a profound disconnect from their emotions, leaving them isolated in a realm of numbness.

Healthy Optimism

The difference between *optimism* and *toxic positivity* rests in how we handle reactions and challenges. Choosing the positive charge of polarity requires emotional fluidity, which occurs when we accept our reality without resisting negative sensations.

We achieve true healing by holding space for unpleasant emotions, allowing them to be processed rather than dismissing reality or rejecting low-vibrational feelings and the experiences of others.

This approach fosters healthy adaptation to challenges, steering us away from old, ineffective coping mechanisms. By embracing this mindset, we cultivate an unbiased perspective that enables us to see the bigger picture, rather than masking despair or self-doubt with distractions.

True inner and outer coherence emerges when we practice authentic emotional transmutation, creating a positive shift without resorting to the "fake it until you make it" mentality.

Each day, we have a choice to show up genuinely and embrace the truth of reality, rather than pretending or living in delusion. We allow our loved ones to express their vulnerable feelings and inner reflections without shaming their experiences. We also accept our own challenges, such as low self-worth, without hiding behind the inability to embrace our natural selves.

A healthy optimistic mindset nurtures vital relationships through understanding and empathy, recognizing the importance of supporting bonds during tough times.

It integrates multiple perspectives, allowing us to take what resonates with our spirit and face challenges with resilience, flow, and growth, rather than reacting with suppression, fear of adversity, and avoidance of the darker aspects of life.

This way, we are aligned and remain open to both the light and the shadows, expanding (positive charge) rather than constricting or shrinking (negative charge) from the fullness of our experiences.

And when we are flowing in true alignment, we are able to navigate stress, challenges, adversities, and life's changes without projecting them onto others. When we face difficulties, even on days with emotional dysregulation, we are still in the midst of integrating our personal healing process.

If we can move through our most stressful moments without letting that process spill over into mistreating others, lashing out, or causing harm, it's a clear indication that we are operating as aligned, conscious, self-aware beings.

Emotional Intelligence

Human emotions are powerful forces that shape how we navigate life, coloring our perceptions and influencing every choice we make. They are not just fleeting reactions to experiences—they are messengers, revealing the deep alignment, or misalignment, between our internal world and the reality we encounter.

Each emotion, whether joy or sorrow, anger or peace, serves as a reflection of our inner state, urging us to pay attention to the unspoken truths within.

But our emotions don't dictate our actions, and they shouldn't hold the reins on our behavior. Instead, they offer profound insights into how we view ourselves and the world around us. They allow us to pause, take stock, and decide how we wish to respond to the patterns.

I realize that this is a key distinction—*reacting on impulse keeps us trapped, but responding with intention liberates us.*

Three core emotions—anger, fear, and sadness—are often at the root of our suffering, making us feel unsafe in our human bodies.

However, these emotions aren't enemies; they are powerful signals leading us back to our authentic selves. They urge us to confront the areas where we have drifted from the unified field of Source consciousness. When viewed through a negative lens, emotions can feel overpowering, but with awareness, they transform into our strongest allies on the journey of healing and self-realization.

This deeper understanding enables us not only to master our own emotions but to steer the emotional landscapes of others with clarity and compassion.

I have learned that mastering emotional intelligence involves navigating the turbulent waters with grace. It begins with self-awareness, the foundation of our ability to choose our responses deliberately rather than reacting out of habit.

With self-awareness comes resilience—the ability to face life's challenges without being overwhelmed, to rise above fear and frustration with discernment and purpose.

Empathy is found at the heart of emotional intelligence, the bridge that connects us to others. It's the ability to step into another's shoes, to understand their pain and joy as if it were our own.

Honing this skill deepens our relationships, allowing us to forge bonds rooted in genuine understanding.
Emotionally intelligent individuals excel in this, handling conflict with compassion, diffusing stress with calm, and communicating with authenticity.

However, our journey doesn't stop there. Embracing our emotions means giving ourselves the space to fully experience them.

Rather than pushing them aside or numbing them, we learn to sit with our feelings, allowing them to surface and flow naturally. This act of emotional release brings balance and peace, integrating these charged energies into a harmonious whole.

Setting healthy boundaries is another essential component. By honoring our own needs, we protect ourselves from emotional burnout, recognizing that we cannot fix everything or everyone.

Boundaries safeguard our energy and preserve the integrity of our well-being, ensuring we remain whole even in the face of others' demands.

Ultimately, emotions are not something to be ignored or suppressed. They are our internal compass, guiding us toward greater understanding of ourselves, our patterns, coping mechanisms, triggers, and the world.

Cultivating emotional intelligence empowers us to harness their wisdom, transforming raw feelings into intentional action and enriching every vital relationship.

For me, sugar addiction has been a coping mechanism to fill my emotional void since early childhood.
While I take full responsibility for what I consume, I acknowledge the struggle of breaking these habits, especially in a world where food is engineered to be addictive. My journey involves a balance between accepting my imperfections and striving for healthier choices on a daily basis.

When we are imbalanced, stagnant, or blocked in our root field, we remain trapped in a perpetual state of conflict and chaos. This keeps us in survival mode, where every situation feels like a threat, triggering fight-or-flight responses.

However, once we begin to heal these foundational third density fears and cultivate a sense of trust and safety within ourselves, we can start to move beyond this reactive way of being.

A balanced root field allows us to feel secure and purpose-driven, transforming life's catalysts from mere survival challenges into opportunities for personal growth and self-realization. We are here to grow, feel, and be real with ourselves.

Once we start meeting our basic needs, our energy can rise to the orange ray—the sacral field—allowing us to process catalysts through personal desires and reactions. This ray allows us to dive into the portal of lessons from each experience to discover their true meaning.

By releasing attachments and embracing an open attitude toward life's catalysts, we allow energy to move past the orange ray to the yellow ray.

The yellow ray, or solar plexus, represents empowerment. When we transcend victimhood, insistence on rigid beliefs, and resistance to reality, we see challenges as opportunities for growth and step into liberation.

The only way to clear and release the survival-based rays is by acknowledging our traumatic events—whether abusive treatment, neglect, toxic relationships, or accidents—they leave deep imprints on our emotional landscape.

Many of us instinctively depress the raw pain of these events as a survival mechanism to carry on with life. This suppression, however, does not erase the hurt; it often magnifies it, causing anger, sadness, and guilt to accumulate as we deliberate on our past.
Thoughts like "I hate what happened" or "I despise that person" weigh heavily on our hearts, creating a cycle of suffering that can linger for years.

As we navigate our lives, the unresolved childhood wounding can manifest as physical dis-ease, or anxiety, depression, and hyper-vigilance.

These emotional wounds may trigger intense feelings, leading to outbursts of anger or pervasive feelings of shame. Many people are struggling to cope, haunted by past memories they wish to forget.

Importance of Healing

To heal and integrate these feelings of pain, we must confront our past and reclaim our emotional well-being:

Acknowledge the Feelings: We begin by reflecting on significant moments in our life that still evoke strong feelings. Identify the emotions associated with these past events. It's important to be real with ourselves and admit if "we still feel sad about our divorce," or "the pain from our childhood still lingers." This act of acknowledgment is the first step toward healing.

Connect with the Body: When we close our eyes and turn our focus inward, we can tap in and locate where these feelings reside in our body. If we understand that emotions are *energy in motion*, then it only makes sense that suppressed feelings will manifest physically. By giving ourselves permission to feel these sensations, we validate their presence with gentle compassion, kindness, embracing our vulnerability.

Replay and Release: If our memories involve being mistreated—or if we have harmed someone—visualize that moment vividly. We imagine having a conversation with that person, allowing pent-up anger or sadness to surface.

We stop fighting the tears, letting them flow freely. When we speak our truth without restraint by expressing our feelings, it's a profound cathartic release. This also activates our throat center.

Conversely, if we are reflecting on treating someone unkindly, we can envision expressing our remorse. We hold space to allow feelings to rise to the surface and to heal, by offering ourselves the grace of forgiveness.

This process of replaying the past in the safety of our inner world is a powerful and courageous act of liberation. Embracing our feelings and articulating our truth opens the door to transformation.

As we confront these memories, we reclaim our narrative and take a significant step toward emotional freedom, paving the way for a more harmonious future.

Releasing Emotional Charge

The art of letting go involves releasing unhealthy attachments, fear, and anxiety, allowing us to realign with our authentic inner feelings. By fostering a sense of inner peace and well-being, we create space for a deeper, faith-based connection to our heart's true desires.

In this state, we no longer chase after external validations—whether it's a relationship, financial success, or physical appearance—believing they are the key to our happiness. Instead, we recognize that fulfillment comes from within.

When we release the need for external conditions to shape our emotions, we begin to understand that true joy, abundance, and love are already present within us. By detaching from the anxiety of yearning, we stop pushing away what we desire and start attracting it naturally.

This shift in perspective empowers us to live in a state of alignment, trusting that everything we need is already available when we tune into our authentic feelings.

Often, we chase thoughts filled with yearning, believing that specific conditions must be met for us to feel love or fulfillment. We might tell ourselves, "I need a particular person or relationship to feel loved," or "I must achieve a certain level of financial abundance before I can feel prosperous."

We may believe that only by losing weight or achieving a specific body type can we finally feel attractive. Perhaps we think that a particular car or a lavish house is necessary for us to feel successful or validated.

What we fail to realize is that by sending out energetic signals of these external needs, we are inadvertently magnetizing and rooted in fear and anxiety. These feelings can create a push-pull dynamic that distances us from what we truly desire.

To transform this pattern, we need to disconnect from these programs that fuel our unhealthy attachments. In these delicate moments, we can affirm, "I feel loved right now." This cultivates the belief that unconditional devotion and acceptance exists within, independent of any peripheral justification.

In embracing this mindset, we step into our sovereign power, shifting our focus to internal harmony. This change in mindset enhances our emotional well-being and attracts the very things we truly desire, allowing them to flow into our life with grace and divine timing.

So, when we understand that the lower aspects of our energy fields are connected to the survival-driven ego, we acknowledge that they operate from a rational, intellectual standpoint rooted in the physical world.

To progress spiritually, it is crucial to balance the root, sacral, and solar plexus fields, allowing energy to rise to the heart, where it merges with universal love, compassion, and a desire to serve the highest good.

Intuition, the counterpart to the ego, arises from the heart's vibratory field, linked to the Infinite Intelligence of Source. It aligns with the third eye energy field, acting as the observer of our higher self and offering a direct connection to universal wisdom.

This guidance system alerts us to negative karma through discomfort, and when the *Coherent Heart* and third eye centers are in harmony, we gain deeper insights and access to the wisdom of higher consciousness.

However, an imbalanced biofield prevents us from feeling clear intuitive signals, often leading us to miss this inner truth due to the distractions of a busy mind. The ego, aiming to suppress intuition, can make it challenging to follow these inner cues.

Thus, the journey that we call the *Hero's Odyssey* to self-mastery, requires us to unblock the lower three rays:

Lack—the primal fear of scarcity and deprivation—originates from our *red root ray*. Overcoming this means nurturing a sense of security and trust.

Attachment—our personal desires and biases—emanates from the *orange sacral ray*. To move beyond this, we need to release our clinging and addiction to the repetitive comforts of suffering.

Control—the urge to dictate life's events—comes from the *yellow solar plexus ray*. The key is surrendering, allowing life to flow naturally without trying to steer every detail.

To reconnect with my intuitive guidance, I have integrated many catalyst experiences and relearned to trust my inner voice. I often ask myself, "What is this feeling trying to teach me? If I strip away fear-based thoughts or programs, what might this sensation be revealing with regard to my vital needs?" This practice allows me to tap into my intuition, quiet the ego's chatter, and navigate life with greater clarity.

By transcending these ego-based programs within our biofield, we align the mind with the heart's energy center and pave the way for growth and upleveling with emotional intelligence.

Musical Tones

I have incorporated the mystical and scientific benefits of the Solfeggio frequencies in my daily healing journey. These ancient musical tones, rediscovered from sacred texts, are believed to hold the key to unlocking our body's natural soothing abilities and balancing the mind, body, and spirit.

Each Solfeggio frequency, like a tuning fork for our soul, vibrates at specific hertz that align with the universal natural rhythms. From 174 Hz, which is thought to relieve pain and stress, to 963 Hz, known as the frequency of divine connection, these tones work on a vibrational level, recalibrating our energy to raise our consciousness.

When we are immersed in a sea of sound, where the hum of 528 Hz—the "Miracle Frequency"—rejuvenates our cells, creating new neuro pathways, it opens our heart field to receive unconditional love from Source. This frequency, long associated with DNA repair, is said to restore our natural vitality.

As we journey deeper, 396 Hz liberates us from fear and guilt, those heavy chains that repress us from our true potential. It's like shedding an invisible weight, allowing us to breathe deeply and embrace the freedom that comes with emotional release.

The 417 Hz frequency, often called the "Frequency of Change," clears negatively charged energy, helping us to move forward to manifest new beginnings.

I have also found that the grounding tones of 741 Hz encourage expression and problem-solving, while 852 Hz attunes us to our higher self, sharpening intuition and opening pathways to higher soundwaves of awareness.

When we align with these frequencies, we sync up with the universe. The vibrations ripple through our being, fostering healing on a cellular level and reconnects us to the pulse of life force energy that flows through everything. With consistent listening, the brainwaves begin to mirror these vibrations, leading to profound states of relaxation, creativity, and spiritual insight.

From my perspective, the Solfeggio frequencies are a vibrational bridge to well-being. Whether we're looking to reduce anxiety, heal from trauma, or simply relax and deepen our meditation practice, these ancient musical tones guide us back to our natural balanced and vibrant state.

Heart-Brain Connection

So now that we are aware that the heart is more than just a vital organ, modern science reveals that it functions with its own intricate nervous system of about 40,000 neurons.

This network senses, processes, and even makes decisions independently of the brain, sending signals through the vagus nerve that deeply influence our emotional, mental, and physical well-being.

I have discovered that scientifically what makes the heart even more extraordinary is the powerful electromagnetic field it generates—the strongest in the body. This field extends several feet beyond us, not only regulating our physiology but also shaping our emotions and thoughts.

When we experience joy, gratitude, or compassion, the heart enters a state of coherence, creating a harmonious rhythm that aligns with the brain and the body.

From a quantum physics perspective, the heart's energy goes far beyond its physical function. It interacts with the quantum field of Source, influencing not just our inner world but potentially the collective consciousness.

From this perspective, the *Coherent Heart*'s neurons are part of a dynamic intelligent system, capable of shaping how we perceive reality through their interaction with the fundamental forces of the universe.

Some believe these neurons operate according to quantum principles like non-locality and entanglement. With this principle, the heart's energy can resonate and connect with people, nature, or environments far beyond our own bodies, intertwining with the fabric of existence in ways we're only beginning to understand.

Over time, as my heart signal grew stronger, my perspective broadened, allowing me to see the world through a clearer, more expansive lens.

As a bearer of light who never quite resonated with the New Age movement, I realized that we don't need to reach the pinnacle of spiritual Ascendent Masters to graduate from this *Angel Academy*. When we leave this Earth, we transform to the next level of higher frequency density.

When we transcend the polarity of judgment and embrace love and acceptance, we enter a new realm of existence. Stepping away from the battle between light and darkness allows the universe to reflect the reality within us. Engaging in causes, such as deforestation, only perpetuates more destruction because, like a hammer seeking a nail, we unknowingly fuel the very forces we seek to change.

I realized that true transformation occurs when we are no longer ruled by lower energy fields. Instead, when we operate from the green heart ray, allowing love and compassion to guide us, we shift our perspective entirely. By harmonizing all six energy fields, balancing opposites, and aligning our actions with this integrated state, we can live a life of deeper purpose, grounded in unity and peace.

It occurred to me that the opposite polarity of unconditional love is conditional love—affection tied to expectations, demands, and judgments. It's based on transactions, offered only when certain criteria are met, creating a façade of acceptance that can easily crumble. While fear and hate often emerge from this dynamic, they are merely shadows cast by judgment.

Conditional love restricts genuine connection, evaluating worth based on arbitrary standards. In contrast, unconditional love is our true essence. It radiates freely, embracing us without reservation and fostering deep, authentic relationships.

This unguarded love is a transformative force, allowing true intimacy and understanding to flourish.

Life is not about being perfect but ensuring that more than eighty percent of the time, our reactions, emotions and actions stem from our heart's intelligence without conditions. This shift to heart-centered being marks the induction of true spiritual intelligence and demonstrates our alignment with the Divine essence.

Self-Love Practice

I have learned that it is so important not to reserve self-love and care only for the times when we are feeling down or overwhelmed.
When we wait until moments of despair to offer ourselves empathy, we create a pattern in the subconscious mind where this practice becomes something we only deserve during hardship.

This approach conditions us to associate love with tragedy, so life starts to feel overwhelming, as though struggle is the only way to access gentle wellness and compassion for ourselves.

To break this cycle, we learn to hold space and practice loving all aspects of our being daily, not just when we are feeling sad or in need of self-liberation.
When we embrace both our highs and lows, we start training the subconscious mind that self-love is not conditional upon distress.

It is an ongoing, unbroken connection to our inner child's innocence, our worth and value, no matter what we are experiencing at the moment.

By loving all parts of ourselves—our joy, creativity, sadness, anxiety, anger, and everything in between—we create a steady flow of Divine devotion that is not dependent on external conditions or emotional extremes.

This practice not only prevents life from feeling like a series of devastating challenges that can overwhelm our senses, but also rewires the mind to understand that pure love is always accessible, regardless of our healing journey.

I have realized that instead of viewing life in a black-and-white, good or bad, high-versus-low vibe manner, this practice of unconditional self-love helps shift our perception to one of wholeness.

It reminds us that every experience, whether light or dark, deserves compassion and care.

I use the practice of self-love to measure how I interact with everything in my life. If something fails to resonate with the unconditional devotion that flows from my *Coherent Heart*, I reassess and integrate it anew.

I remain mindful of the self-critical, judgmental, negative, insecure, or fearful thoughts that occasionally creep into my mind. In those moments, I practice forgiveness—both for these thoughts and for myself—allowing them to dissolve through the healing process.

When we accept and love all parts of ourselves, it helps us live in harmonious alignment with our true essence, where we embody love consciousness in our daily routine.

It becomes the foundation of our existence, not just an emergency measure for when we are in crisis mode.

Spiritual Intelligence

Metaphysical wisdom suggests that our ability to understand and integrate life experiences is a direct reflection of our spiritual intelligence. This is activated by the heart's emotional intelligence, the opening of the green ray and living from the space of individualized free will.

This deeper awareness allows us to perceive the lessons within our challenges and to apply this knowledge for personal growth. By aligning with this wisdom, we can navigate life with greater clarity, purpose, and a deeper connection to the divine essence within us.

We can achieve spiritual intelligence when we blend self-awareness and embodiment with harmony. It is the mastery of our inner knowing, combining the masculine and feminine aspects of our being—represented by the left and right hemispheres.

This expansion of consciousness is a real and measurable process linked to awareness. To tap into this evolution, we must understand the nature of reality, heart and mind coherence, and the role of ego.

Consciousness expands through the union of the masculine (self-awareness) and feminine (embodiment) energies. Together, they help us comprehend reality by transcending the filters of ego, conditions, beliefs, and traumas that cloud our awareness.

To evolve spiritually, we must process and integrate catalysts—those challenging experiences that trigger growth—*by navigating the pathway embedded in our first six energy centers, which serve as processing centers for consciousness.*

As our spiritual intelligence ascends through the energy network along the spine, it reaches the seventh ray, the crown field. This is the gateway to Infinity—the divine intelligence of Source that is available within us, only when we unlock this key to our higher self. This requires us to recognize our true essence by balancing all six energetic fields within our biofield.

This can be measured by how well we process life experiences through all six energy centers, with each field equally engaged in this catalytic progression.

There are specific qualities within these centers that reflect our embodiment and integration as complex, multi-dimensional beings, helping us gauge our level of spiritual growth and mastery.

We get there by awakening the heart intelligence, living from the heart field, the fourth green ray. When every experience flows seamlessly through the lower rays, the heart becomes the bridge connecting us to the higher centers as we respond with empathy and understanding.

Once our awareness is centered in the crystalline heart, we see every circumstance through the lens of compassion, transforming life's catalysts into opportunities for personal growth and self-realization.

When we achieve a *Coherent Heart*, we elevate our awareness to the throat field, the fifth blue ray, where catalysts are integrated with wisdom and insight. Here, we begin to perceive deeper metaphysical connections and synchronicities in our lives, understanding the universal intelligence operating behind everything.

As we advance to the third eye, our sixth indigo ray, we gain mastery over catalysts, becoming psychically attuned to the thoughts and emotions of others. This stage represents a deep connection to the quantum field, opening the gateway to Infinite Intelligence.

The final stage of self-mastery is reaching the crown's violet ray, the seventh energy field, where we experience the singularity of Source consciousness, also known as the higher self.

We embody divine intelligence and access profound knowledge and wisdom in harmony.

Balancing our energy centers to reflect the original harmony of the Divine's golden light is vital. Each of us has a unique rhythm, even though we share the same energy centers: red, orange, yellow, green, blue, indigo, and violet.

Our biofield's auras reflect which energy fields are activated through the toroidal flow. Our distinctive balance might emphasize different rays, depending on our path and purpose.

Imagine a pattern of energy so fundamental that it weaves through every facet of existence, from the smallest atom to the vast galaxies. This is toroidal flow, the continuous, self-sustaining dance of energy that moves in a circular loop, expanding outward, only to return to its source. It's a motion within our biofield that defines balance, unity, and infinite regeneration.

At its core, toroidal flow is a dynamic vortex. Energy flows outward from the center, curving around to the edges before spiraling back inward, forming a shape reminiscent of a cosmic doughnut.

This endless cycle of expansion and contraction mirrors the breath of life itself—a constant exchange between what lies within and the world beyond. It is a pulse, a rhythm, a heartbeat that beats across the cosmos.

In the physical world, we see toroidal patterns in magnetic fields, from the Earth's protective magnetosphere to the electromagnetic field surrounding our human heart. These invisible waves of energy shape our reality, creating the balance that holds life together.

But beyond the physical, toroidal flow exists as a universal principle, embodying the harmony between the inner and outer worlds, the seen and unseen.

If we picture the energy that surrounds us, circulating in perfect synchrony, we realize that it is the life force that moves through our body. It spirals through the heart center, expanding our awareness, and reconnecting us to the Source of all creation.

This flow not only sustains life but also serves as a reminder of the interrelation of everything. Every thought, every feeling, every action we take moves through this energetic system, contributing to the whole.

I realized long ago that the toroidal flow is more than just a concept; it is a living reality. When we attune ourselves to it, we feel the truth of our existence—that we are both creators and receivers, giving and receiving in a continuous loop of energy.

It's a mirror of our personal growth, where every challenge we face is an opportunity to expand, and every return to the center is a chance for renewal.

In the grand scheme of the universe, the toroidal flow represents the infinite cycle of life. There is no beginning or end, only the eternal exchange of energy. It shows us that no matter how our souls traverse the densities, we are always connected to our origin, always drawn back to the center of ourselves.

This is the fundamental essence of being—a flow of consciousness, constantly evolving, constantly returning to the Source.

The torus is the ultimate symbol of balance—a perfect fusion of motion and stillness, of evolution and accord. It is the blueprint of life itself, a powerful reminder that we are not separate from the universe but an integral part of its unfolding design.

When we align ourselves with this flow, we step into the natural rhythm of creation, allowing the energy within us to manifest our highest potential. *This electric pulse is the heartbeat of the universe—and it beats within every one of us.*

Our biofield also represents the Divine Creator's golden Logos that was expressed into seven energy rays, which must be balanced, just as it was originally split.

Rather than trying to activate each center fully, the key is to harmonize them, like tuning an instrument such as a harp. Every string must be in sync to produce a beautiful chord.

When our energy fields are out of balance, we generate a discordant note, creating feelings of discomfort.

SEVEN DENSITIES

The seven octaves or densities represent stages of frequency of our consciousness and spiritual evolution, guiding the soul toward ever-deepening self-awareness and unity with the Divine.

Each density reflects a different level of illumination, where we evolve through energetic frequencies, spiritual intelligence, awareness, sovereignty, and choice:

First density: The level of *basic existence* and awareness where consciousness emerges through the elements of the physical plane—earth, water, fire, and air—where existence revolves around survival and the awakening of the simplest form of sentience. It is the initiation of consciousness in physical form.

Second density: The level of *growth and development.* It is associated with plant and animal life, where sentient beings start to develop a rudimentary sense of identity, though they act largely on instinct.

The lesson of second density is about learning to respond to stimuli and gradually expand a sense of self. Here, existence is driven by primordial instinct and emotional awareness, activating only the lower two energy centers—the root and sacral fields—allowing them to respond to their environment and develop rudimentary alertness.

Third density: The level of *self-awareness and choice.* The majority of humans in the world exist in third density, where the core lesson is about making conscious choices, often between service to others (unity) or service to self (separation). This density represents a major shift in consciousness, as individuals begin to understand free will, morality, and the illusion of separation from Source.

In contrast, third-density beings develop full self-awareness through the activation of the solar plexus, or yellow ray in the material world. This energy center is the foundation of human consciousness, enabling lessons, reflection, perceptions, choice, and understanding of the self. It is a journey to learn how to love and receive love.

It encompasses the physical, emotional, and mental bodies, anchored in the root, sacral, and solar plexus fields, which define human experience. As we move through this density, we grapple with a false belief system, making choices between service to self or service to others consciousness.

The mirage of separation from Source consciousness is the fabricated conviction that we are isolated, disconnected beings, cut off from the divine energy that flows through all life. Source consciousness is the infinite awareness, the creative force, the essence that binds and sustains everything in existence.

When we identify solely with our physical form, ego, and the material world, we lose sight of this deeper connection. We start to see ourselves as separate, distinct from others and the universe, which can lead to feelings of seclusion, dread, and a sense of lack. This perceived separation fuels competition, judgment, and suffering because we forget the truth of our interconnectedness with all living things.

Currently, humanity and the planet are undergoing a profound shift in consciousness, transitioning beyond material third-density into a higher-frequency reality. This evolution echoes the structure of the seven densities, which align not only with our energy rays but also with the colors of a rainbow and the notes of a musical scale.

Fourth density: The level of *love and understanding*. In the fourth density, we begin to develop a deep awareness of unity and interconnection. This density focuses on collective consciousness, lessons, compassion, and healing.

In the fourth density, the *Coherent Heart* becomes central. Humans begin to recognize the interrelation of all life, transcending and serving others as they move beyond ego-driven desires.

Fifth density: The level of *wisdom and balance.* This stage is about the refinement of understanding and Gnosis. In the fifth density, we use inner knowledge to focus on deep introspection and develop clarity of thought. When we operate from the fifth density, heart-mind coherence takes precedence, as humans learn to balance in harmony. This is a stage of self-mastery and embodied understanding, aligning our spiritual intelligence with the Infinite Intelligence.

Sixth density: The level of *unity consciousness.* In this density, we have integrated both love and wisdom and are learning to transcend duality. We experience the Oneness of all things, having a deep understanding of creation and the interconnected nature of reality.
By the time consciousness reaches the sixth density, love and wisdom are fully embodied. It is understood that spirits who transcend duality may become guides to those in lower densities.

Seventh density: This level is about *completion and dissolution*, where the soul's individuality begins to dissolve as it prepares to merge with the totality of existence. It represents the return to Oneness, Source or Infinite Intelligence, having completed its evolutionary journey of expansion.

This density marks the culmination of spiritual transformation, where the soul transcends the need for further individual experience and growth.
The soul returns back into the Logos, contributing to the continuous cycle of creation, development, and evolution.

From my perspective, the seven densities represent our soul's journey through stages of consciousness, or higher frequencies, each one deepening our awareness of existence. This metaphysical structure allows Infinite Intelligence to experience itself through these octaves of awareness.

Each density contributes to our evolution in every form of life, and as we progress from this physical world, we gain a greater understanding of our divine essence and the unity of all existence.

Ultimately, we are all on Earth to anchor our enlightened divine essence, our spirit, within human experience. The Divine Creator or Source unfolds through us as we navigate the spectrum of life through our coded cellular memories stored in the universal archives.

All our challenges, pain, joy, loss, heartbreak, worry, growth, and bliss we encounter—it's about learning love, treasuring experiences, and cultivating a harmonious unity within ourselves and in our relationships.

From my perspective, when our time comes to transform from this density, only pure love endures, leaving an eternal radiant footprint of our presence.

This process expands our consciousness on this extraordinary planet, grounded in the beauty of Mother Earth. When she suffers, we suffer, for all life forces are interconnected in this intricate web of existence.

This realization shifted my view into one of gratitude—not to escape reality, but to integrate its contrasts with the sacred light of loving awareness.

Insights into the Nature of Self

In my exploration of esoteric wisdom, I have discovered that the higher-self of Source expression orchestrates experiences and catalysts to help me polarize during my lifetime on Earth. It gently nudges and guides me while respecting my free will as a dream character.

My true essence is not broken or fragmented, it's already complete and whole; I'm merely in the process of remembering the truth of my divine expression.

Creation, as I see it, is a fractal of nature—a grand expression of the same Divine blueprint, the Logos, manifesting at various scales, from galaxies to the first physical forms.

From an esoteric perspective, the Logos embodies the fundamental principle of order, reason, and creative expression that permeates the universe. Often linked to the concept of original thought of Source, it serves as the essence through which all creation emerges. It signifies the intricate interplay between consciousness and matter, acting as the guiding blueprint for existence. Rather than a mere philosophical concept, it is a living force that imbues the cosmos with meaning and purpose, inviting individuals to align with this higher wisdom to discover our true nature and potential.

The universe itself functions as a network of intelligent relationships, illuminated by the golden hues of the Logos—a nonphysical state of consciousness. Each layer of creation reflects a distinct aspect of this Source relationship, shaping reality at its own scale and transmitting the blueprint into physical manifestations, revealing the interconnectedness of all existence.

Just as galaxies and stars possess unique structures with free will to explore and create in natural Divine Order, planetary bodies evolve based on their chemical structures. Each level of creation operates as its own microcosm.

We often ponder the purpose of life and our reason for being here. The Universal Law of Oneness reveals that there is one divine Source of eternal life force energy, an Infinite Intelligence within the quantum field.

This Source, devoid of contrast, created physical reality to experience itself, mirroring its own omnipresence. *We are the mirrors through which Source sees its reflection, expressing itself through our physical forms and states of consciousness.*

Our consciousness vibrates and spirals through dimensions, accessing higher realms by releasing energetic attachments to lower densities. As I heal blockages within my seven energetic fields, often referred to in my poetry as colored wheels or rays, I transition to different wavelengths of awareness through the veil of forgetfulness.

The pain-body, formed from concentrated negative energy of the ego-self, or survival mindset, signifies stagnation or imbalance in my life force energy, especially when I neglect to heal my inner child.

This disconnection from divine wholeness results in suffering, and as my energetic biofield becomes more fragmented, I experience increased polarization or contrast, leading to defensive, angry, or negative reactions that further entrench my misery.

This is the law of cause and effect, or karma. The more polarized karmic imprints we generate, the deeper our suffering becomes in this physical reality.

Our energy centers generate emotions through vibrations, reflecting our state of consciousness, whether blocked or openly flowing within our auric biofield. Emotions act as a feedback loop, revealing either positively or negatively charged frequencies.

We now understand that emotions are genuine, non-conceptual experiences that arise from the core of our being. Suffering often stems from rejecting these feelings, particularly those labeled as negative, such as anger, sadness, and fear. However, fear itself does not cause suffering unless it is ignored or deemed undesirable.

These sentiments need to be acknowledged, processed, and expressed openly, just as we accept the natural process of breathing. Unprocessed emotions can intensify over time, often triggered by trauma or distressful catalysts from intense life events.

It is vital to recognize that true healing involves embracing, processing, releasing and integrating these emotions through acceptance, vulnerability, and compassion.

Our world is in disarray because of the collective energy we emit, rooted in the negative charge of judgment. At its core, this cognitive process involving evaluation and interpretation often leads to negative emotional responses, which can manifest as sensations in the body.

It is the act of forming opinions or conclusions about people or situations, often shaped by our personal beliefs and experiences.
It ranges from neutral observations to harsh criticisms and reflects the moral frameworks we carry—defining what we perceive as right or wrong, good or bad.

These judgments, though sometimes subtle, are heavily influenced by our biases and cultural conditioning, often creating division and fueling discord.

When we judge others or situations through a lens of separation and superiority, we reinforce negative energy that clouds our perception of unity. The more we feed into this mindset, the more fragmented and chaotic our world becomes.

This process has a profound negative impact on both our inner and outer world. When we judge, we create a separation between ourselves and others, reinforcing the belief in superiority, inferiority, or biases.

This perspective not only distances us from unity but also triggers a cycle of negativity. Since judgment stems from unresolved inner conflicts or insecurities, it acts as a form of self-attack, amplifying feelings of inadequacy or fear.

On an energetic level, judgment emits a low vibration, which, according to the principle of "what we emit is what we receive," attracts more negativity into our lives. This can manifest as inner suffering—self-doubt, guilt, or frustration—and external conflict, as judgmental thoughts and actions often lead to strained relationships, misunderstandings, and emotional pain.

Over time, judgment can distort our perception of the world, blinding us to possibilities, growth, and the empathy needed for true connection.

To shift this, we must replace judgment with observation, acknowledging that every individual and circumstance is part of a much larger, interconnected whole.

Having healthy curiosity as a neutral observer radiates a positive charge, fostering growth and understanding.

From my level of awareness, belief in separation from Source arises from the mortal mind, where lack or deprivation, attachment, and control outline the unholy trinity of the survival-based ego.
When I view myself as a fragmented entity from the Divine, I struggle with feelings of unworthiness, cling to

external factors, and try to control outcomes out of fear and self-judgment.

The narratives and stories we create stem from these egoic limiting belief systems.

I have come to understand that all the love, peace, harmony, and joy I seek are already encased within my human form, the nature of self. There's no need to search for an external savior or to find someone else to complete me.

When we are aligned and in a flow state, perfectly balanced in our solitude, we naturally magnetize an alchemical counterpart if that is our heart's desire.

However, we can only experience this profound connection when we are united in mind, body, and spirit, embracing our sovereignty and readiness to receive with an open, Coherent Heart. In this state, our energetic expression becomes genuine and transparent.

In my daily practice, I cultivate inner tranquility by finding peace in my heart center and releasing a mindset of scarcity. *Living with a lack mentality fosters feelings of desperation, victimhood, and insecurity, which are mirrored in our external reality.*

By recognizing myself as an expression of Source creation, I aim to embody love and the true essence of wholeness and sacred light, which reveals a deep inner peace.

Once we achieve this state of inner calm, we cherish and protect it, accepting our authentic, quirky selves and our peaceful surroundings, regardless of external conditions.

Inner peace brings a sense of harmony where worries and fears diminish, allowing our mind to be clear, our emotions balanced, and our connection to a deeper purpose or understanding strengthened.

Peace often brings quiet joy, grace, and a sense of completeness to a world filled with conflict and chaos. In this state, we vibrate at a higher frequency, emitting dharma—positively charged waves of light—that helps illuminate the world's shadow aspects, to alchemize karmic imprints and integrate generational trauma.

By following this practice, we acknowledge and release darkness or shadow aspects back into the original blueprint of Source consciousness to be transmuted.

Humanity's karma or dharma is shaped by our individual and collective actions, thoughts, beliefs, and feelings, creating a pattern for our ascension and potential, or descension timelines.

When we observe negative thoughts without acting on them, we prevent the creation of new karmic ties, allowing us to break free from cycles of suffering. The more we practice this action, the more dharma we create. *And this is the concept of self-mastery.*

The universe acts as a mirror, reflecting the state of our mind and vibratory emittance. When we perceive reality as separate from Source, our ego uses suffering as a mechanism to challenge our understanding of truth.

The body, in this context, serves as a learning device, a sacred vessel through which we experience and grow, but it is not the essence of who we are.

We are non-physical beings of pure consciousness, transcending the limitations of our physical form. And energy cannot be destroyed, just transformed.

Our true nature is not defined by the labels that society imposes upon us—this branding often lead to dehumanization, fostering division, and manipulation in the service-to-self path of competition, judgment, greed and corruption.

This path uses language, money, and deceptive propaganda as tools to control and divide, brainwash, creating enemies among us. However, these labels make a false impression, masking the truth of our shared existence and the unity that binds us all.

I have often pondered the deeper meaning of the Luciferian beliefs, service-to-self archetype, and the concept of evil. I dive deep into these views and share my knowing of polarized entities in my *Ascending Angel Academy* series with fictional storytelling.

This narrative represents the timeless cosmic ancient battle between unity and separation, the duality of light and dark, coherence and chaos.

In this framework, God or Source is seen as the pure, unified, omnipresent sacred light—the ultimate source of love and Oneness that permeates all existence. This divine consciousness operates under the law of unity, where all beings are interconnected and part of a singular divine essence, the Logos.

Evil or Satan, in contrast, is viewed as the archetype for the human ego in the physical realm, embodying fear, and shadows of suffering, through the veil of amnesia. This energy is associated with oppression and the distortion of truth with sin-based beliefs, often referred to as the "trickster" archetype.

Dogma and man-made belief systems invert our true existence, promoting a false light narrative of external deities that enforces hierarchy and sin-based programs. The divide and conquer tactics of the overlords, and the belief that we are inherently less than fosters apprehension, and hate, distorting our natural unity.

The matrix of our world, which means "womb" in Latin, is built upon this illusion of separation as it exists in this belief structure. It manifests in the controlling systems on Earth—such as the political, banking, pharmaceutical, food, religion, and oil industries—that seek to dominate and manipulate to maintain overlord powers.

These archaic systems thrive by perpetuating drama, disease, disempowerment, with confusing narratives to pit us against one another. To break free from this cycle of chaos, we must remember to reclaim our sovereign power using discernment and realize our self-mastery.

Honest self-examination is essential for understanding our beliefs and sharpening our discernment. Joy is our birthright, yet we mistakenly believe it must be earned through struggle. Challenges, approached with curiosity, can become opportunities for growth rather than sources of suffering.

If we shift our perspective, these obstacles can be like puzzles, offering a sense of accomplishment and expanding our knowledge and skills. By overcoming them with curiosity, we not only enrich our own lives but also inspire others to see that fulfillment doesn't have to come through hardship.

I have realized that sometimes, souls choose to enter physical reality with disabilities or diseases—not as punishments, but to provide humanity with lessons and opportunities for healing. These advanced souls often take on challenges to help others discover cures or develop new approaches to overcoming obstacles.

What may seem limiting on the surface can be a profound act of service, inviting us to view constraints through a lens of optimism and innovation. In this way, hardships can transform into powerful catalysts for collective growth and evolution.

Self-Mastery

Engaging on the path of radical self-mastery is the profound journey of understanding and aligning with our true essence. It involves integrating our ego and shadow-self with devotion and taking radical accountability for our behaviour. We take control of our emotions, and actions, transcending limiting beliefs, and aligning with our higher self.

Through inner work, meditation, and conscious living, we harmonize our mind, body, and spirit, achieving a balance and wisdom that reflects the divine within.

This mastery empowers us to navigate life's challenges with trust, grace and authenticity, contributing to both the personal and collective evolution.

The path to healing the world rests in recognizing each other as a mirror of Source, Infinite Intelligence and embodying the eternal truth of our divine nature. This is how we can transcend the illusions of the physical matrix and restore balance and peace to the dualistic world.

I realize that the concept of time, like death and separation, is a trickster construct—fears masked by the linear paradigms of the mind. From my perspective, all that exists is the infinite and eternal now, where our energetic expressions cannot be destroyed.

Existence is a continuous flow of energy. Without time, the notion of death dissolves, revealing that change is the only constant in existence. Embracing this reality dissolves any apprehension of mortality, allowing us to live fully in each moment.

LAWS OF THE UNIVERSE

Reality mirrors our consciousness, and Source, in its perfect wholeness, embodies omnipresence, strength, and eternal abundance.

The universal Source is an infinite being that knows itself through our existence, while the ego thrives on dualities like pleasure and pain, chaos and coherence, creating impressions of deprivation and fear of impermanence.

Our time, lessons, and experiences in this physical reality prepare us for the "great event," the evolution and transformation of our awareness for the next expression of our essence through levels of density.

When we truly integrate this universal knowing, what remains is pure love and harmony, reflecting our true nature. This realization fosters a life of profound peace, beauty, and gratitude, where boundaries of time, death, and separation dissolve.

Will we graduate from the angel academy of Earth or repeat the same dimensional grade through reincarnation?

We may discover our answers by understanding the Laws of the Universe. *Just as every wave is an expression of the ocean, every action in the cosmos reflects the spirit, guided by both physical and spiritual order.*

This metaphor reminds us that we are vital parts of a greater whole, in a harmonious relationship with the rhythm of existence.

The metaphysical principles that govern the nature of reality, nature of self, and how energy shapes our experiences include:

Law of Oneness: Everything in the universe is interconnected and originates from the same Source. All beings, matter, and energy are part of a unified whole. I put this understanding into action by recognizing that everything is a relationship and choosing to hold space for my loved ones with empathy. This commitment deepens the bonds that connect us, fostering a sense of community, unity, and shared purpose.

Law of Vibration: Everything in the universe vibrates or pulses at its own frequency, including thoughts, emotions, and physical matter. Higher vibrations attract a positive charge, while lower vibrations draw a negative charge.

I put this principle into action by immersing myself in inspiration—whether through nature, creative outlets like writing and artwork, or uplifting company. I choose to surround myself with optimism and hope, flowing in artistic expression with enthusiasm.

Law of Attraction: Like attracts like. The energy we emit, through thoughts, feelings, and actions attract experiences that match that frequency. I put this into action by radiating gratitude and aligning with inner peace, magnetizing the energy into my auric field. I begin each day with affirmations, feeling the joy of my present moment that's already manifested. I AM worthy, I AM safe, I AM powerful.

Law of Cause and Effect (Karma): Every action has a corresponding reaction. Positive actions yield fulfilling outcomes, while negative actions result in challenges or lessons. I embrace this principle by choosing to react with kindness and compassion, knowing that my generosity sets in motion a wave of goodwill. When I emit from my heart field without any expectations, it is magnified back into my biofield.

Law of Correspondence: The patterns and laws that govern the macrocosm (the universe) are reflected in the microcosm (individual experience). As within, so without; as above, so below. I put this transformation into action by cultivating clarity through meditation and self-reflection. When chaos reigns in my external world, I turn inward, to align and balance my thoughts and emotions, with a *Coherent Heart.*

Law of Polarity: Everything exists in pairs of opposites, revealing that these contrasts are not separate but intertwined facets of the same reality. Light and dark, hot and cold, love and fear—all are expressions of a singular energy, differing only in their vibration and frequency. Embracing this principle enhances my awareness and empowers me to navigate life's complexities with grace.

When faced with challenges or catalysts, I understand they are opportunities for growth, and that pain often precedes healing. By recognizing both sides of any experience, I cultivate balance and harmony in my life. This duality invites me to shift my perspective, urging me to focus on the positives even in adversity.

Through this lens, I come to appreciate the full spectrum of existence. Each challenge becomes a steppingstone for personal transformation, fostering strength and insight that reshape my understanding of hardship. In this way, I learn to thrive amidst life's contrasts, emerging more resilient and enlightened.

Law of Rhythm: Life unfolds in cycles, much like the changing seasons, the phases of the moon, or the rhythmic ebb and flow of the ocean. Everything moves in harmonious rhythms, and change is the only constant. I embrace this universal flow by acknowledging that both growth and rest have their own seasons.

In times of low energy, I give myself permission to disconnect, recharge, and reflect. I understand that these moments of introspection are essential for renewal. By committing to daily acts of self-devotion, I align myself with the natural rhythms of life, fostering balance and harmony within.

This trust in the cyclical nature of existence empowers me to navigate each phase with grace, ensuring that I am prepared to blossom anew when the time is right.

Law of Gender: Both masculine and feminine energies exist in everything. These forces represent creation and balance, and they work together to manifest reality. I put this into action by embracing my divine alchemical union—not seeking externally for someone to complete me. I live authentically with softness and grace, cultivating creativity and intuition alongside action and logic.

I activate my voice to stand up for myself with integrity, recognizing when to push forward and when to surrender, creating harmony in my life and decisions.

Law of Perpetual Transmutation: Energy is in constant motion, forever shifting and transforming. It emphasizes that energy cannot be destroyed; rather, it perpetually changes form, impacting our reality in powerful ways.

Consider how potential energy becomes kinetic energy when an object is set in motion, or how emotional energy can be expressed through creativity in art or music. This principle serves as a powerful reminder that we hold the ability to change our circumstances by consciously directing our energy and focus.

When I learn to shift negative thoughts into positive actions, I harness the power to transmute what no longer serves me into something beautiful and life-affirming. I reshape my experiences and align my deepest desires, paving the way for personal growth and a life filled with purpose, joy, and fulfillment.

Law of Relativity: All experiences are qualified, based on our perceptions and understandings which are shaped by the context in which we find ourselves. This helps us gain an outlook by observing trials and situations from a broader framework. This law helps us view our challenges as part of a larger perspective.

I have realized the Law of Relativity unveils a profound truth about our human experience: *the significance of any moment is intricately woven into the fabric of comparison.*

For example, how do we feel when joy erupts like a brilliant sunrise, illuminating our hearts after the heavy, gray clouds of sadness have passed? The dance between contrasting emotions transforms the ordinary into the extraordinary, shaping our thoughts, emotions, and perceptions in a way that makes us acutely aware of the depth of our existence.

When we consider the power of perception—what feels like a crippling obstacle to one may be viewed as a golden opportunity for another. This subjective lens through which we interpret life's events reflects our unique histories, beliefs, and experiences. It's a reminder that our emotional landscape is as diverse and multifaceted as the people who inhabit it.

Understanding Truth

The concept of a single objective truth suggests that there exists an absolute reality, a fact that stands independent of personal beliefs and experiences.

This notion implies that, regardless of individual interpretations, certain truths remain universal and unchanging. However, this idea often clashes with the rich complexity of human emotion and experience.

Our understanding of truth is shaped by the myriad experiences we encounter. Two individuals can witness the same event, yet emerge with entirely different narratives, colored by their emotions, beliefs, and life stories.

This subjectivity challenges the existence of a singular objective truth, prompting us to explore the nuances of perception.

I recognize that cultural and contextual influences further complicate our understanding. Each society upholds distinct values and beliefs that shape its interpretation of reality. What one culture may embrace as truth can be viewed through a contrasting lens in another, highlighting the diversity of human reflection.

Moreover, our comprehension of truth is not static; it evolves over time. Scientific discoveries and societal shifts can transform what we recognize as "the truth," revealing that our interpretation is in constant flux. As we grow, our perspectives change, encouraging us to question previously held beliefs.

Emotions, too, play a vital role in our perception of truth. Feelings can intensify certain experiences, making them feel profoundly true to us, even if they diverge from a more objective standpoint. This emotional lens adds depth to our understanding, reminding us that truth can be as much about the heart as it is about the mind.

Ultimately, the interplay between objective truth and subjective experience invites us to embrace a more intricate view of reality.
While certain facts may exist independently, the essence of human experience lies in our diverse interpretations.

Recognizing this complexity fosters empathy and understanding, enabling us to appreciate the rich tapestry of existence while simultaneously seeking the universal truth of balance that bind us together.

We often define our reality through the interplay of opposites, navigating a world where light is understood against the backdrop of darkness, love resonates because of the contrast with judgment or hate, and success is illuminated by the shadows of failure.

This constant comparison enriches our understanding and deepens our emotional resonance, inviting us to explore the depths of our feelings.

Embracing the Law of Relativity grants us a remarkable gift—the power to shift our perspectives. When we acknowledge that our challenges are not fixed but relative, we unlock the potential to transform our mindset.

This newfound clarity empowers us to approach difficulties with resilience and creativity, turning each setback into a stepping stone toward growth. In this way, we become the architects of our own reality, capable of navigating the complexities of life with strength and grace.

By aligning with these universal principles, we can create greater harmony and influence our reality with intention. *Everything is interconnected and shaped by these fundamental laws of existence.*

Karmic Imprints

I acknowledge that many see Karma as a form of punishment, but from my perspective, Karma helps us achieve balance and growth.

The law of cause and effect isn't about judgment—it's a neutral force that ensures we evolve and ascend.

When we disrupt the universal laws energetically, the consequences we face are not punishments but opportunities for growth and deeper contemplation. In the grand Divine Design of love consciousness, nothing is random.

Every challenge or setback becomes a doorway to expansion, offering us insight into our own nature and the intricate web of interconnectedness that binds all things. Even our missteps carry purpose, revealing the reality that everything unfolds in alignment with a higher, intentional order.

Though we may choose to act against these laws, we cannot escape the outcomes that follow. These consequences serve as vital reflections, showing us the very essence of the laws that shape our reality. They are necessary for us to grasp the underlying framework of Infinite Intelligence that permeates our existence.

Without these reflections, we would remain unconscious of the profound structure that governs the universe and guides our journey of self-discovery.

The Law of Cause and Effect is an unbreakable thread woven through the universe. Every action, whether charged positively or negatively, creates imprints or a ripple that inevitably returns to us.

Positive actions bring forth positive outcomes; negative actions lead to challenges that push us to learn. Within this divine system, karma becomes our most profound teacher, continually offering us chances to evolve.

When we shift our mindset, we begin to see our journey as a continuous unfolding of countless lessons, each one enriching our understanding of life. Each experience becomes a steppingstone, guiding us through the complexities of existence, and revealing the wisdom hidden within our struggles.

By acknowledging this progression, we cultivate resilience and a deeper appreciation for the journey itself, recognizing that every lesson is a vital part of our evolving story.

If we refuse to learn from them, we'll face them again—perhaps in another lifetime of equal density—until we're ready to ascend to the next level of consciousness.

Karma, then, is not a concept of retribution. It's the universe guiding us, always encouraging us to grow in balanced harmony, to move toward higher states of awareness.

Process of Renewal

To achieve harmony and balance, we must unite both divine masculine and feminine energies within our biofield.

The feminine moves through sensation, with art, and expression, weaving life from the rawness of experience. It doesn't simply create—it initiates, treating each moment as sacred.

For women, the descent into the body is a rite of passage as a creator of life, a journey toward awakening.

Many of us have lost touch with the profound reality that society has historically stifled the feminine spirit. We have been taught that embracing the full power of our bodies is unsafe. This shame and distortion trap us in chaos, often manifesting as body dysmorphia, disconnecting us from our essence.

We become ensnared in our thoughts, held captive by external influences, suffering in this disconnection—until a fire within stirs, urging us to rise from the ashes.

In this awakening, our *Organic eMotions* become our compass, guiding us through the labyrinth of our knowing. Our bodies transform into a map, leading us on an exhilarating adventure of soul evolution. Unfortunately, there are no shortcuts; we must brave the dark unknown. Yet the feminine thrives in community, nourished by breathwork, sound, and movement.

As we journey inward, we confront the profound knowing of our soul. This remembrance ignites every cell, initiating a powerful reawakening. We come to understand that the path forward leads us into the vast, uncharted space where our vision of the highest potential exists alongside the friction of our misaligned inner and outer worlds.

In this crucible of change, the process intensifies, compelling us to grow, dismantle old patterns, and reorganize our lives in alignment with our vision of self-actualization.

Life responds, orchestrating events, lessons, and experiences perfectly calibrated to pull us closer to our highest vision. Along our *Hero's Odyssey*, forgotten aspects of ourselves are retrieved, and we come alive in our full spectrum, igniting new possibilities and harmonizing with the rhythms of nature.

The process of renewal transcends mere reclamation of the past; it is a powerful journey of resilience and integration, a rebirth into a state of balanced wholeness with every breath we take.

This emerging version of ourselves embodies the potential the world craves—the one who perceives a vibrant vision, embraces the unknown, and transforms aspirations into tangible reality.

As this embodiment strengthens, it generates an unshakable force field. In uniting the logical mind of our masculine with the creative force of our feminine, we birth new timelines for ourselves and the collective.

Across the planet, women are rising, walking through the path of fire, alchemizing pain into power, reclaiming the feminine essence, and embracing the golden glow of wisdom and potential.

A new era is unfolding—one where we remember who we are and embrace the magic we have always carried within our light codes.

Bodies of Consciousness

I understand that consciousness expresses itself through our seven energy fields, each radiating its unique vibration. When the lower three energy centers become blocked, my essence is ensnared in a downward spiral, caught in the third density of suffering.

Here, the **physical body** serves as our gateway to existence, immersing us in a rich tapestry woven from the dualities of life—pain and pleasure, joy and sorrow, life and death. Within this sacred vessel, we confront the stark realities of our existence, including the undeniable beliefs of physical mortality.

Yet, the tangible realm often traps us in a cycle of victimhood, where we feel helpless against the currents that sweep us along. But a shift is imminent. When we awaken to our inherent power as co-creators, we shatter the confines of this mindset. We learn to harness our ability to shape our experiences, seizing control of our destiny in every fleeting moment.

Beyond this physical form lies the **subtle body**, a realm of vibration and mental perception where thoughts, emotions, and astral journeys entwine. It beckons us on a profound quest of self-discovery, guiding us back to our Soul—our truest essence—through practices like meditation and deep introspection. Here, we unearth the forgotten truths of who we are.

Transcending the subtle body invites us to recognize our connection to the Universal Mind, the Infinite Intelligence that pulses through all of creation. This awakening urges us to transcend individual limitations, merging with the vast interconnected web of consciousness that cradles us all.

As we journey deeper, we encounter the **causal body**, where profound meditation and deep sleep transport us to realms of bliss and emptiness. In this sacred space, we shed the dualities that define our waking existence, unearthing the serenity that resides within pure consciousness. Here, harmony reigns, unfettered by the chaos of our daily lives.

To transcend the causal body is to awaken to the essence of pure consciousness—the ultimate reality. It is a domain of unbroken unity and boundless bliss, aligning us with the eternal wisdom of who we are. In this expansive state, we break free from the constraints of form and identity, allowing us to bask fully in the radiant light of our being.

Each breath becomes a celebration of our journey, a testament to the limitless potential that unfolds as we navigate the intricate dance of existence.

As we transcend the **dream state**—whether through the subtle body or the unconscious realms of the causal body—we often find ourselves ensnared in a dance between attachment and resistance. These forces keep us bound to the cycle of duality, swinging between the extremes of positive and negative experiences.

Awakening to our divine essence means moving beyond these extremes, finding balance within. This transformative process involves shifting from conditioned reasoning to the illuminating light of awakening—a state where we recognize our true nature as unified beings of consciousness.

In this awakened state, we are no longer bound by the illusions of the mind but are aligned with the truth of our eternal Oneness with all that is.

We emerge from the shadows of duality, embracing the harmony that lies at the heart of our existence.

Universal Consciousness

As we rise from the shadows of lower realms, our awareness attunes to the luminous frequencies of the quantum field. This sacred journey calls for a bold embrace of responsibility, urging us to shed the burdens of blame and reclaim our power as sovereign beings of divine wholeness.

In this transformative alchemy, we fuse our personal, sexual, and spiritual identities into a harmonious tapestry of acceptance, devotion, and love. We become living reflections of the universe, each of us a unique expression of the Divine.

Forgiveness emerges as a vital force in this process—not just a release, but a profound awakening to our eternal essence. By recognizing that the actions of others stem from their own inner struggles, we transcend the illusions of separation that the ego clings to.

To truly forgive is to understand the motivations behind others' actions, allowing the weight of past grievances to dissipate like fog in the morning sun. This doesn't mean we condone their behavior or minimize the pain inflicted. Rather, it acknowledges a shared humanity where hurt people often project their suffering onto those around them.

Yet, true forgiveness represents a courageous refusal to be shackled by the pain of others. It rises above judgment, granting us the freedom to unearth the roots of our suffering. From a place of compassion, the *Coherent Heart* enables us to sever the invisible threads binding us to past hurts, freeing the negative charges trapped within our energetic fields.

This release transforms pain into healing, guiding us toward a state of balance and harmony.

In the universe, feminine and masculine energies coexist in perfect equilibrium. When we judge others, we anchor ourselves to the same negative frequencies, trapping our spirits in a cycle of discord. Liberation is impossible while we remain ensnared in this mental labyrinth.

By choosing to release judgments, we de-polarize our minds, illuminating the shadows within and contributing to a collective transformation. We become beacons of hope, illuminating the path for others who seek to rise.

Within this web of interconnectedness, our consciousness intricately weaves the fabric of our physical and energetic realities. By cultivating inner harmony, we align ourselves with the vibrational currents necessary to manifest our desires.

Each deepening breath in meditation raises our vibrations, offering clarity and access to higher realms of peace and bliss.

Ultimately, this journey reveals the essence of universal consciousness—pure love in its most radiant form. We evolve into anchors of unity and harmony, not just for ourselves but for the entire world.

In this state of being, we heal not only our wounds but also the collective pain of humanity, intergenerational wounding patterns, igniting a timeline shift that reverberates through every heart and soul.

Shifting our Vibration

When we experience low vibe or negatively charged emotions, they can affect our well-being and alignment with spiritual intelligence.

We understand that negative emotions can act like shadows, lurking beneath the surface and influencing our lives in profound ways. **Sadness** wraps around us like a heavy blanket, often triggered by loss or disappointment, leaving us feeling isolated and hopeless.

Shame stings deeply, whispering lies about our worth, and pushing us into silence, while **guilt** traps us in a relentless cycle of remorse, feeding our anxieties.

We have all felt the wrath of **jealousy**, a fierce fire ignited by insecurity, making us feel inadequate as we watch others thrive. **Envy** festers like a wound, as we compare ourselves to those who seem to have it all, pulling us further away from our own joy.

Frustration bubbles beneath the surface, a tension that escalates into anger when we hit walls that block our paths. **Disgust** can turn our stomachs, making us recoil from unpleasant experiences and tainting our relationships.

Loneliness seeps into our bones, a painful reminder that we can feel utterly isolated even in a crowd. **Hopelessness** clouds our vision, leaving us adrift in despair about what the future holds.

Regret haunts us like a ghost, whispering about choices we wish we could undo, while **self-doubt** gnaws at our confidence, stifling our dreams and ambitions.

Recognizing these emotions is the first step toward liberation. By confronting them with courage and compassion, we can begin to dissolve their power over us. Through mindfulness, therapy, and self-reflection, we can transform these shadows into stepping stones, creating a brighter, more authentic path toward emotional resilience and fulfillment.

Without dissolving these negatively charged emotions, we continue to exist emitting a **low vibe.** This state is characterized by the dense, heavy energy, and a sense of disconnection from Oneself and the world. It can manifest as a lack of motivation, chronic stress, or an overall feeling of being "stuck."

Low vibrations often correlate with thoughts that are self-critical or pessimistic, leading to a mindset focused on lack rather than abundance. We may feel overwhelmed by life's challenges, trapped in polarizing thought patterns, feeling completely isolated from reality.

Living at a low vibe can affect not only our emotional health but also physical well-being, contributing to stress-related ailments, burn-out, and diminished energy levels. It creates a cycle where negativity breeds more negativity, making it difficult to see the potential for joy or growth.

However, I have learned that it is possible to shift from a low vibe to a higher vibrational state through practices such as mindfulness, self-care, and engaging in activities that promote positivity, connection, and self-acceptance.

By consciously choosing to work on elevating our vibratory field, we have the power to transform our experiences, improve our outlook, and cultivate a more fulfilling life.

When we have a high vibe, we are resonating at a higher *vibrational* state, radiating positive energy, and aligning with emotions like joy, love, gratitude, bliss, and inner peace. It is a state of emotional and spiritual elevation where we feel connected to ourselves, others, and the world around us.

It reflects a sense of harmony, balance, and flow, where challenges are met with resilience, and opportunities for growth are embraced with optimism.

In this elevated state, our thoughts are more focused on abundance rather than lack, and we naturally attract positive experiences. We feel empowered, clear-minded, and energized, able to move through life with a sense of purpose and ease.

From my perspective, having a high vibe also deepens our connection with others, fostering relationships that are nurturing and fulfilling. Our viewpoint expands, allowing us to see the beauty and potential in everyday moments.

Physically, the higher *pulse of movement* often leads to greater vitality and overall well-being. It's a state where we are more mindful, creative, and attuned to the present moment, cultivating gratitude for every breath. By living in this elevated vibrational state, we are co-creating a reality filled with possibilities, peace, and alignment with our higher self.

Having a high vibe resounds the I AM projection from our level of awareness as aspect of Source consciousness, devotion, and spiritual wisdom.

Frequency, however, is the measurement of *how fast or slow that energy pulses*. It represents the degree at which a vibration occurs, defining its unique rate and energetic signature, much like our heartbeat.

Higher frequencies indicate quicker, lighter energy, often associated with higher awareness, while lower frequencies are slower, denser, and tied to material or ego-driven states.

When we attune our subtle bodies of light with the supreme vibration of Source Divinity, we raise our sentience frequency.

In short, vibration refers to the type of energy, while frequency indicates the rate at which that energy moves or oscillates, with both factors influencing our spiritual and emotional experiences.

So, having a high vibe indicates that we have processed and integrated our shadow aspects, allowing us to oscillate at a higher rate of frequency. This state is aligned with positive emotions such as love, joy, empathy, forgiveness, peace, and bliss.

It reflects an elevated awareness, connecting us to our true nature, fostering balance and harmony with the world. We begin to attract positive experiences and radiate uplifting energy to those around us.

Resonance happens when matching frequencies align, amplifying each other's energy in motion and creating deeper connections and harmony.
This interplay of vibration, frequency, and resonance illustrates how all elements of existence interact, influence, and enhance each other in the cosmic dance of energy.

How do we raise our frequency? In my experience, meditation or deep contemplation, is a powerful practice that transforms the mind, body, and spirit by fostering relaxation, mental clarity, and emotional balance.

It quiets the mind, reduces the inflammation of stress, and dissolves negative thought patterns, leading to a more peaceful and focused state of being.

By enhancing self-awareness and deepening our connection to our true self, intentional reflection unlocks inner wisdom and intuition. With regular practice, we cultivate and amplify resilience, flow, and creativity.

Ultimately, meditation is the doorway to personal growth, spiritual awakening, and experiencing the Infinite Intelligence within us, guiding us toward the realization of our highest potential. As we exist in this flow state, our frequency naturally rises, allowing us to navigate life's challenges with greater grace and inner peace.

As our level of consciousness rises, so too does our energetic vibration. For example, love and inner peace resonate at a frequency of 500 hertz within the body, mind, spirit complex, and when we reach this rate of occurrence, we gain access to blissful realms or heaven on earth.

Karmic law compels us to confront and heal the trauma-based suffering and shadow blockages to which we are attached. To heal from the law of cause and effect, we must retrieve the energy we have extended outward through resistance to life.

Forgiveness, surrender, soul retrieval, and non-attachment are essential practices for this healing process, leading to self-actualization and the full realization of our divine essence.

This understanding inspires compassion and helps us release our chains to the pain or suffering caused by those actions. By embracing these practices, we dissolve karmic ties, breaking cycles, and move closer to our true nature—pure love and unity with Source.

When we trust in our soul's vibratory essence, we embody the universal consciousness of pure love.

Earth, as I see it, is like a school for celestials—a space for higher dimensional beings to incarnate and expand our awareness in this density. It is here that we transmute negative polarity into positive wavelengths, serving love and shifting our evolution toward harmony and unity on this beautiful and magical planet.

It is my understanding that all forms in the universe are extensions of Source, yet the Source itself transcends all forms, binding everything together in eternal unity.

I have always known this as love consciousness, which reflects the unique fingerprint of every spirit, that is connected and exists in an intricate relationship with all other forms of existence.

Just as a puzzle piece belongs to a larger whole, we are simultaneously both the part and the whole. *We are a unique expression of Source, and at the same time, Source is expressed through us.*

This duality reveals a profound correspondence, showcasing the art of self-actualization. It encourages us to see the Divine presence in everything and to understand our eternal connection to it.

By embodying this awareness, we harmonize with the universal flow of love, wisdom, surrender, and unity, unlocking our highest potential as spiritual beings.

Ultimately, the *Hero's Odyssey* requires the reclamation of our free will through our heart field, the dissolution of fear-based regimes, and the conscious choice for inner peace. We can choose to live in coherence with the sacred light of unity by focusing on our inner alignment and balance.

Using our Free Will

Activating the *Coherent Heart* allows us to harness the profound power of free will—the ability to shape our lives through conscious choice, beyond the grip of fate or external forces.

It is a Divine gift that allows us to navigate through life based on our own intentions, desires, and actions, rather than being completely governed by preordained forces.

Free will exists as a key principle in many metaphysical frameworks, particularly in relation to spiritual growth, karma, and the evolution of the soul.

In this context, *free will is viewed as a sacred tool for soul progression or expansion*—each decision we make reflects the choices of our inner being, influencing our vibration, reality, and future.

Through free will, we are given the opportunity for radical accountability, to learn, grow, and experience different aspects of existence, often encountering catalysts that challenge us to align with our higher self or remain in states of fear, limitation, or ego-driven desires.

While we may face certain circumstances or conditions set by Universal Laws or soul contracts, *free will gives us permission to choose how to respond.* It empowers us to co-create our reality in collaboration with the universe and Divine Will.

The choices we make, consciously or unconsciously, set into motion the energy that shapes our experiences and defines our journey toward self-actualization.

Surrendering to the Flow

Surrender is an act of cooperation. To truly surrender, we must stay attuned to life, listening to the moments when life calls for our participation.

I have discovered that life itself is a dynamic relationship, especially as we move into fourth-density consciousness, where a loving connection with existence becomes essential.

Life invites us to deepen this relationship, much like a surfer harmonizing with the ocean. In this metaphor, the

surfer waits for the perfect wave, positioning themselves with patience and focus.
When the moment arrives, they paddle with determination to catch the wave's momentum, and once caught, the ocean's energy carries them effortlessly forward.

This is how we are meant to engage with life—staying present, seizing opportunities when the time is right, and trusting that the flow will support and guide us.

Existence and Bliss

Reality, when freed from the mental projections we impose upon it, is pure bliss. The essence of existence in Sanskrit—*Sat, Chit, Ananda* (Existence, Consciousness, Bliss)—is the true nature of all that is.

When I published *The Joy of I.T. (Infinite Transcendence)*, I realized that within the unified quantum field, where everything is interconnected, there is no war, strife, or conflict; there is only absolute, unbreakable harmony.

As I tapped into creative flow, I aligned with my higher self and entered this state of bliss. It is the organic, natural condition of Source consciousness, the fragrance of the One Creator that lacks absolutely nothing.

Upon recognizing our true nature as expressions of the infinite, eternal, all-pervading, and all-knowing, the concept of fear dissolves, since it cannot exist within this frequency.

I have found that profound inner peace is a reflection of how deeply we have realized our Oneness with Source, the pure love awareness that transcends all illusions of separation and lack.

This peace isn't something to seek or strive for—it is an intrinsic quality of our being, accessible when we understand and embody the truth of who we are.

Anything that deviates from love, harmony, or perfection is merely a mental projection, not reality. By dissolving these illusions, we return to *Ananda*, the natural state of bliss consciousness, where we fully embrace the eternal, unchanging presence of Source within us.

Polarity's Path to Wholeness

Polarity is the cornerstone of our universe, a fundamental force that governs the ebb and flow of existence through electromagnetic energy.

At its essence, polarity operates through two opposing yet complementary forces: the positive (electro) and the negative (magnetic). The positive polarity embodies radiant, unifying, and creative energy, acting as a force of light and expansion.

In contrast, the negative polarity represents chaos, absorption, and entropy—a state of increased randomness and disorder. However, rather than viewing the negative polarity as something to be feared or eradicated, it's crucial to understand its role as a catalyst for growth, evolution, and transformation.

It took me a while to comprehend that darkness is not the absence of light. *From the lens of physics, darkness is the absorbed condition of light.*

The concept of darkness and the shadows of the ego are not adversaries to be vanquished; they are parts of us that need to be integrated and loved back into wholeness.

Love, in its purest form, is a force that builds, heals, and harmonizes, while fear serves to separate, divide, and destroy.

Yet, it is often through the darkness that we are pushed towards our inner light. *Negative polarity, therefore, is our catalytic teacher.* It is guiding us through the challenges of life so we can emerge stronger, more unified, and more aligned with the ultimate truth that positive polarity embodies.

By embracing both light and darkness within us, we achieve a deeper understanding of our true nature and move closer to completeness.

Contrast

If we understand that consciousness evolves through seven densities, then each must represent stages of growth, where higher densities offer more light to fully express and understand.

Our planet, now in the third density, is transitioning through polarity—a crucial phase in our collective evolution. By raising awareness of light, we elevate the planet's frequency, aligning with a shared destiny of service and unity.

Polarity, a fundamental metaphysical law, *balances positive and negative energies in the universe, driving growth through contrast.*

We understand *space* as the vast, seemingly infinite expanse that surrounds us, representing the potential for creation and the void where possibilities arise. It acts as a canvas for consciousness, allowing energy to flow and display in *various forms of substance.* Space invites contemplation of our relationship with the universe and the significance of our presence within this expansive reality.

Material form embodies the physical manifestation of matter, encompassing both objects and living beings. From an esoteric viewpoint, this tangible world serves as a temporary expression of concentrated energies of consciousness, reflecting higher realms of existence.

While the physical realm is ever-changing and impermanent, it offers profound insights into the nature of reality and our interconnectedness with the universe, inviting us to explore how our experiences in material density can illuminate our spiritual journey.

In this polarized universe, space represents negative polarity, while form embodies the positive. Together, they create a dynamic balance. Understanding contrast as a catalyst for evolution helps us transcend fear, realizing that negative polarity reflects the opposite, what the Creator is not.

Instead of resisting negativity, we can transmute it through love, using it to reveal our own light.

Polarity acts like an electromagnetic force, with positive energy building, unifying, and creating, while negative energy absorbs and dissipates.

This balance is crucial—darkness cannot be destroyed by hate, only integrated with our sacred life force energy. Love, the ultimate positive force, harmonizes and heals, while fear separates and destroys. Our shadow selves compel us to seek light, and negative polarity, as the ultimate teacher, drives us toward balance.

As we grow more self-aware, old ego-driven patterns may resurface, tempting us to revert to familiar thoughts of fear and separation. However, to continue evolving, we must release these outdated patterns and align with our *Coherent Heart*, transcending negativity.

Polarity teaches us that both light and dark are necessary for the full experience of existence. Integrating both brings us closer to realizing our divine nature and the unity that underlies creation.

Our journey to wholeness involves balancing masculine and feminine energies—masculine seeks truth and action, while feminine embodies intuition and creativity. Harmonizing these contrasts allows us to navigate life with purpose and alignment, embodying wisdom with grace and clarity. Through this integration, we align with higher states of consciousness, creating a life rooted in love, harmony, and spiritual evolution.

Flow of Giving and Receiving

The universe operates as an endless flow of giving and receiving, a dance of energy that reflects the inherent nature of Oneness.

All things exist in relationship to one another, and even the ego, with its tendencies towards separation, cannot escape this fundamental truth.

Recognizing Oneness involves striving to make all of our relationships loving and harmonious, understanding that the energy we put out into the world is the same energy that will return to us.

Humanity's evolution depends on raising our spiritual intelligence to match our technological advancements. Without pure love, even the most sophisticated technologies like AI can become destructive forces that consume our human essence rather than elevate it.

Relationship with Money

Money is a powerful form of energy that represents freedom to express our heart's desires. However, our relationship with money often reflects deeper beliefs about abundance, scarcity, and self-worth.

To align with the truth of our being, we must remove limiting beliefs around lack and scarcity, recognizing that abundance is the natural state of reality and our inherent nature.

True universal wealth comes not from the accumulation of material possessions but from understanding and embracing the boundless abundance that is available to us in every moment.

We must embrace the belief that we are inherently worthy and recognize that our time and energy hold immense value. When we understand our worth, we set boundaries, make empowered choices, and align ourselves with experiences and relationships that uplift and nurture us.

This self-awareness is key to living a life of purpose, where we invest our energy or focus wisely and trust that we deserve love, respect, and fulfillment. Only by valuing ourselves can we fully honor the gifts we have to offer the world.

By cultivating a healthy relationship with money, we open ourselves to the flow of abundance, allowing us to live in alignment with our highest purpose and express our divine essence freely.

Embodying Our Limitless Being

Human Incarnation

The journey of human incarnation is a sacred and reflective experience, where the divine essence within us chooses to enter the physical realm, navigating the complexities of life on Earth.

From my level of understanding, it involves confronting the veil of forgetting—a profound spiritual amnesia that momentarily hides our connection to our true divine essence.

In the physical realm's space-time matrix, this forgetting is crucial for our evolution, as it sets the stage for self-discovery and growth. Without the veil, there would be a shortage of challenges and catalysts that inspire us to seek deeper truths, rediscover our inner light, and ultimately align with our higher self.

This temporary disconnection is not a flaw but a necessary part of the soul's path toward self-mastery.

By engaging in life's lessons, challenges, and experiences, we are given the opportunity to realize our complete potential, to remember our divinity, and to awaken to the truth of who we really are.

Each incarnation is a unique and invaluable chapter in the soul's ongoing journey toward enlightenment as we navigate the intricate tapestry of existence. Here, consciousness can be understood and measured in terms of rays or energy fields, each corresponding to one of the seven densities.

These energy centers, often depicted as colored wheels, represent different levels of awareness and spiritual evolution. The third density, where most of humanity currently resides, is characterized by self-awareness, personal identity, and the challenges of duality.

However, as we strive for Oneness and unity of self, we begin to transcend the limitations of this density, evolving to higher levels of consciousness where the focus shifts from self-service to service to others.

This evolution is not just a metaphysical concept but an energetic reality—a vibrational match to our spiritual growth in this Golden Age. As we ascend through these densities, our awareness expands, and we become more attuned to the interconnectedness of all life, participating in the greater cosmic dance of the multiverse.

Integrating the Higher Self

The rise of consciousness is not a race to shed the false layers of our being but a journey of embodying and integrating the vastness of our higher-self into our human experience.

We are eternal beings, living on Earth for a fleeting moment to realize and actualize our soul's infinite potential.
The process of fully embracing our higher-self spans countless lifetimes, as the magnitude of our true nature is beyond the capacity of any single existence.

True growth requires the courage to open our minds and accept this perspective, to embrace our eternal presence, and to cultivate a lion-hearted spirit that rejects the urge to play small.

It is through this integration that we begin to live in alignment with our limitless essence, expanding our consciousness and allowing our divine nature to manifest itself in every aspect of our lives.

Nature of Reality

Reality, in its purest form, remains unchanged regardless of our perceptions, thoughts, or beliefs. Our essence is inherently perfect, and when we deny or resist our true nature, we create a rift between divine truth and illusion.

An awakened mind transcends this duality, becoming serene, graceful, and humble, fully immersed organically in the present moment.

I realized that the *Hero's Odyssey* was not about escaping reality but recognizing and aligning with its unchanging nature. In this orientation, we find peace, joy, and the realization that love and balance are the only reality.

From a metaphysical perspective, *reality* is not just the physical world we see but a complex interchange of energy, consciousness, and perception.

Everything that exists, from thoughts to emotions to material objects, is fundamentally energy vibrating at different frequencies.

This energy is shaped by our consciousness, meaning that our beliefs, intentions, and awareness directly influence the world we experience.

The importance of alignment rests in how we harmonize with the universal flow of this energy. When we are in alignment with our true self—our higher self,

representative of divine consciousness—we resonate with frequencies of love, peace, and abundance.
In this state, we attract positive experiences, manifest our desires more easily, and live in greater harmony with the universe. Alignment is the key to unlocking our potential, as it allows us to act from a place of authenticity and purpose.

When we are out of alignment—whether due to fear, doubt, or ego-driven choices—we create resistance, experiencing stress, conflict, and obstacles. This misalignment distorts our perception of reality, leading us to feel disconnected or trapped in lower vibrational states.

By realigning with our higher self, we dissolve these blockages, allowing the flow of energy to support our growth, healing, and evolution.

Ultimately, reality is a reflection of our inner state. The more aligned we are with love, balance, and unity, the more our external world mirrors this harmony back to us.

Alignment is essential not only for personal fulfillment but for contributing to the collective vibrational upliftment of humanity and the planet.

Freedom

The notion of freedom is not a destination to be reached but an objective truth to be unveiled. We are not liberated by acquiring our autonomy; instead, we are born into it, confined only by the illusions spun by our own minds.

At its essence, the nature of reality is freedom itself, and as we strip away these self-imposed veils of belief systems, we reclaim our natural state of liberation.

The external world serves as a mirror to our internal landscape; when we view it through the lens of love, harmony, and purity, we reconnect with our true essence.

Just as the vast depths of the ocean exist beyond the surface waves, and the sky exists beyond its clouds, our core self transcends the transient nature of thoughts, emotions, and material manifestations.

As embodiments of Source energy, we possess the key to freedom within the present moment, where we are already whole, complete, and sovereign.

By recognizing this inherent truth, we empower ourselves to live authentically, embracing the fullness of our being and the boundless potential that exists within.

Purification

On my path to self-realization, I have discovered that the concept of healing is not about changing who we are but reviving the innate purity nestled within our inner child—an essence that is limitless, perfect, creative, and free.

It's a journey of allowing our true selves to emerge without judgment or resistance. By embracing this childlike innocence, we reconnect with the core of our being, peeling away the layers of conditioning that have dimmed our inner light.

True healing emerges from the acceptance of ourselves as we are, freeing us from the need to alter or suppress any part of our being. It is a return to the wholeness that is our birthright, a reclamation of the joy and authenticity that once flowed effortlessly within us.

THE MYSTERIES OF THE HUMAN BODY

An Interconnected System

The human body is a remarkable and interconnected system, operating as an intelligent network where each part collaborates in perfect harmony. This intricate web highlights the significance of viewing health holistically rather than as isolated components.

I have come to realize that when one aspect falters, it sends ripples through the entire organism, revealing the delicate balance required for overall well-being.

At the heart of this system is an incredible communication network. The nervous system relays rapid signals, allowing for immediate reactions to external stimuli, while hormonal pathways manage longer-term processes like growth and metabolism. Together, they orchestrate a symphony of responses that keep the body adaptable and responsive to its environment.

Central to maintaining this equilibrium are feedback mechanisms, which monitor and adjust bodily functions to ensure homeostasis. For instance, I have discovered that when blood sugar levels rise after eating, the pancreas secretes insulin to bring those levels back down.

Conversely, if they drop too low, the body activates processes to release glucose, exemplifying the incredible precision with which our systems operate.

In many holistic practices, such as Traditional Chinese Medicine, the concept of Qi—vital life force energy—flows through the body along specific pathways. Maintaining a balanced flow of Qi is essential for health since disruptions can lead to illness.

Ancient practices like acupuncture and meditation promoted this energy flow, fostering harmony within.

The interdependence of bodily systems underscores the connection between physical, emotional, and spiritual health. Chronic stress, for example, can trigger inflammation, impacting the immune system and creating a cycle of distress. On the other hand, physical ailments can affect mental well-being, reinforcing the need for a comprehensive approach to healing.

Over the years, I have found that fostering resilience is another hallmark of the human body. When faced with challenges, such as illness or injury, it activates repair mechanisms, engaging the immune system and initiating tissue regeneration. This adaptability is a testament to our inherent strength, allowing us to navigate life's complexities.

Ultimately, the human vessel strives for self-regulation. The process of homeostasis is our body's remarkable ability to adjust our internal environment, ensuring stability and optimal functioning in response to both internal and external changes. It is constantly working to create a balanced environment.

Through this intricate interplay of systems, we are reminded of the importance of nurturing every aspect of our being—physical, emotional, and spiritual.

By recognizing how our choices and lifestyles impact this dynamic network, we can cultivate a life of health and harmony, embracing our true potential.

When harmful substances disrupt this balance, it signals internal conflicts and disparities. I recognize that these disruptions provides insight into our body's state, allowing us to make informed choices that cultivate optimal health.

When I align with my life force energy, I tap into my innate potential for well-being and vitality. This allows my intelligent body to self-regulate at the cellular level, harmonizing my physical, emotional, and spiritual aspects.

Schumann Resonance

In recent years, awareness of the Schumann resonance has surged, highlighting its profound effects on our planet and human consciousness. Named after physicist Winfried Otto Schumann, this phenomenon refers to Earth's natural electromagnetic frequency, primarily oscillating between 7.83 Hz and 60 Hz.

From my perspective, this resonance is created by the relationship between lightning strikes and the Earth's surface. It reverberates like a vast cavity between the planet and the ionosphere, influencing the vibrational frequencies of all living organisms, particularly our DNA.

Our human cells function as fractal antennas, receiving and processing information across a spectrum of frequencies. This capacity allows DNA to respond to biochemical signals as well as broader energetic influences, including electromagnetic fields and cosmic energies.

As the Schumann Resonance fluctuates, it stabilizes our biological systems, aligning our physical and energetic bodies with Earth's natural rhythms.

The rise in our planet's frequency fosters a collective positive shift, enhancing our overall well-being and nurturing a deeper relationship with Mother Earth.

Consider the following steps to align with the Schuman Resonance:

Align with Natural Rhythms: I make it a point to spend time in nature, whether it's a walk in the park, hiking, or simply sitting outside.

Being Mindful: Being aware of my vibrational frequency has become a part of my routine. I engage in practices like meditation, radical affirmations, prayers for humanity, and maintaining healthy boundaries to keep my energy elevated.

Support Collective Evolution: I choose to participate in activities and community practices that promote collective harmony. Whether it's through Soul Tribe prayers and intention setting, environmental efforts, or the renewal of Earth's electromagnetic fields with grid work, I know that these actions contribute to both my personal shift and the planet's transformation.

Integrating these concepts into my daily life has allowed me to navigate relationships with more balance, well-being, and contribute meaningfully to collective evolution.

It's a continuous journey of aligning with natural rhythms and supporting the greater good, which enriches my life and the world around me.

Universal Flow and Relationships

When we contemplate the areas of our life where these principles can be applied, we explore how they might transform our understanding of self and our relationship with the universe.

This reflection is an invitation to deepen the connection with our true nature and to embrace the path of spiritual evolution with an open heart and mind.

The universe operates as an endless flow of giving and receiving, reflecting the interconnected nature of Oneness. All things exist in relationships, and even the ego is bound by this universal law.

Recognizing Oneness involves striving to make all relationships loving and harmonious. Humanity's evolution depends on raising our spiritual intelligence to match our technological advancements. Without love and compassion, artificial technology may consume our essence, leading to a disconnect from our true nature.

By embracing the law of giving and receiving, we align with the natural flow of the universe, fostering balance and coherence in all aspects of our lives.

Embracing Human Integration

An integrated being honors the full spectrum of human emotions, recognizing them as sacred elements of our journey rather than obstacles to bypass.
Instead of trying to "kill" the ego-mind, we are invited to fully embody our higher selves, anchoring our wisdom and light into our physical reality. This expression calls us to live from a place of love, allowing us to accept all human experiences with an open heart.

Integration is essential for achieving inner harmony and spiritual awakening. This process isn't about escaping the human experience; it's about fully embracing it. As we anchor our light bodies and allow our higher selves to guide us, we discover that enlightenment emerges from living authentically, with love as our core energy.

This journey of acceptance and self-awareness nurtures our wholeness, teaching us to balance our divine nature with our human existence.

At the heart of this transformative journey is the path of service, where true spiritual evolution unfolds.
The highest expression of our divinity manifests in serving others—offering compassion, wisdom, and kindness without expectation or attachment.

Love emerges as the most potent force in the universe, a boundless source of harmony that guides us toward unity consciousness. By dedicating ourselves to the path of service to others, we align with the ultimate truth: love is the foundation of collective transformation and ascension, leading us all toward a higher state of being, where each of us shines as a beacon of light in the tapestry of existence.

Directing our Attention

By focusing on expanding self-awareness, healing, and integration, we empower ourselves to live in coherence with our highest potential.

Conversely, focusing on negativity binds us to the artificial matrix of hate, fear, manipulation, deception, and confusion. This is where we experience mental health, anxiety, depression, and dis-ease within the body.

When we direct our attention intentionally, we amplify our capacity to learn, understand, and retain information. Whether studying for an exam, engaging in a conversation, or practicing a skill, focused attention enhances our ability to absorb and process knowledge.

This happens when our brains can only fully engage with a limited amount of information at once. By narrowing our focus, we create a mental environment conducive to clarity and understanding.

Moreover, the energy we invest in our attention influences the outcomes we manifest. In metaphysical terms, *where attention goes, energy flows*.

This principle suggests that by focusing on positive intentions and goals, we can attract corresponding experiences into our lives.

For example, when we consistently direct our attention toward personal growth and self-love, we begin to embody those qualities, fostering a transformative shift in our mindset and interactions.

Additionally, attention and focus play a critical role in emotional regulation. When we consciously choose where to direct our thoughts—be it gratitude, compassion, or affirmations—we can alter our emotional landscape.
This practice empowers us to respond rather than react to external circumstances, promoting resilience and inner peace.

In essence, cultivating the power of attention and focus allows us to reclaim agency over our lives. It invites us to consciously choose what we engage with, shaping not only our personal realities but also the collective experience of existence.

By harnessing this power, we can navigate life with intention, creating pathways toward contentment, connection, and a deeper understanding of our true selves.

This empowerment through attention is the key to healing our inflamed nervous system, living a life of purpose, balance, freedom, and fulfillment.

The Power of Divine Union

This concept represents a powerful transcendence that merges the sacred aspects of ourselves with the greater cosmos, creating an exhilarating connection to all that exists.

At its core, this union harmonizes dualities—spirit and matter, masculine and feminine—leading us into a holistic experience of love and unity that resonates deep within our souls.

Sexual energy is a vital force in this transformative journey, propelling our spiritual evolution and influencing our ascension. When this energy is exchanged for mere superficial pleasure, it can pull us to lower frequencies, slowing our vibrational growth.

Conversely, when directed into divine union, this energy accelerates our spiritual development, transforming our nervous system and igniting euphoric bliss. This sacred practice honors the integration of our polarities, allowing the masculine and feminine within us to unite and flourish.

In engaging with divine union, we unlock a profound understanding of our interconnectedness. This connection elevates our consciousness, revealing the illusion of separation and showing us that our individual journeys weave into a grand tapestry of existence.

It fosters a deep sense of belonging and purpose, empowering us to contribute meaningfully to the collective whole.

Moreover, divine union serves as a catalyst for personal transformation. By respecting the sacred nature of sexual energy, we align with higher frequencies of love and unity, enhancing our journey toward enlightenment and self-realization.

At a broader level, divine union signifies the ultimate goal of our spiritual evolution—the return to Oneness with the Source. This journey involves shedding layers of ego and illusion, allowing our souls to merge with universal consciousness. Through practices like meditation, prayer, and acts of service, we cultivate this union, experiencing profound connections that elevate our lives.

Manifesting Desired States

We shape the reality we desire by fully embodying it in our thoughts, emotions, and actions. If we yearn for a life brimming with peace, we must first cultivate that peace within ourselves and express it outwardly.

This journey begins with the heartfelt act of sharing our essence with the world, rather than simply wishing for what we want and envisioning the desired outcome.

To manifest a reality that aligns with our deepest desires, we must first give that energy into the universe. It's not enough to merely ask; we must engage in a reciprocal flow, as outlined in the Law of Giving and Receiving. By radiating our intentions, we create a harmonious connection with the universe.

I realized that the real enigma we must resolve for ultimate creative power in our lives is that giving and receiving are one of the same. This perspective challenges the conventional view that these two actions are separate.

In the realm of energy and Law of Attraction, they are intrinsically linked; when we give selflessly, we open ourselves to receive abundantly.

By embodying the spirit of generosity, we create a flow of energy that enhances our connection with the universe. This exchange not only nurtures our own growth but also enriches the lives of those around us.

When we offer love, kindness, and support, we cultivate fertile ground for our desires to be manifested into our reality. The act of giving ignites a cycle of reciprocity, drawing in experiences and opportunities that mirror our intentions.

Recognizing this unity allows us to transcend the fear of lack and embrace a mindset of abundance. As we give freely from our hearts, we become magnets for the very blessings we seek.

Thus, the paradox dissolves: in our willingness to give, we find the key to receiving the boundless gifts of life. By understanding that these two forces are intertwined, we unlock our true creative potential, harmonizing our existence with the rhythms of the universe.

This alignment unlocks our heart portal, allowing divine love to flow through us. When we consistently act in ways that reflect our highest aspirations, we attract experiences that resonate with our true essence.

This powerful manifestation process becomes a catalyst for co-creating a vibrant life filled with joy, abundance, and fulfillment, guiding us toward the reality we envision.

Transcending Linear Time

Through metaphysics, I discovered that the soul experiences time vertically, while the ego perceives it horizontally. Embracing timelessness opens our heart to the natural flow of love, which moves effortlessly through the present moment.

Trusting in Divine Design and practicing forgiveness help us transcend linear time, leading us into an upward spiral of eternity. By shifting our perception of time from a linear to a vertical experience, we align with the eternal nature of our being, where past, present, and future converge into a single moment of now.

From a metaphysical perspective, the present moment is a powerful convergence point where all possibilities exist, representing the eternal now. It transcends the confines of linear time, blending past experiences with future potential into a continuous flow of awareness.

This dynamic space is not just a fleeting instant; it is a profound opportunity for creation and transformation. Here, awareness connects with its highest potential, revealing deep insights and fostering a sense of unity with the universe.

It is also a profound invitation to live fully and consciously in the present.
By embracing mindfulness, shifting our viewpoint, connecting with natural rhythms, and exploring our sentience, we can unlock the freedom to exist beyond the confines of past and future. When we receive the magic of the present moment, our life unfolds in extraordinary ways.

This transcendence of linear time allows us to live in harmony with the flow of the universe, where every moment is an opportunity for growth, healing, and expansion.

Integrating Philosophy into Daily Life

Before we can transcend our human limitations and ego-based survival instincts to manifest our desired reality, it's essential to nurture a healthy relationship with our distress patterns and mental health.

I often tune into my three lower vibrational energy centers—root, sacral, and solar plexus—to assess where my reactions originate, as these rays govern survival, emotions, and personal power.

By acknowledging and integrating these energetic imbalances, we can heal, dissolve, and break free from reactive behavior.

This conscious effort elevates our awareness and aligns us with the deeper purpose of our *Coherent Heart*, empowering us to create a life of intentional harmony.

Understanding Suffering

When we react from an ego-driven attitude, we get trapped in cycles of attachment and resistance—either chasing external validation or running from discomfort.

In this state, insecurities and distress rise to the surface, fueled by a sense of victimhood. By denying our true emotions, we sever the connection to our authentic selves, distancing ourselves from the inner peace we seek.

This is how we spiral into suffering—by rejecting, judging, denying pain or resisting real feelings, especially those tied to fear, sadness, and anger. True healing begins when we embrace our emotional states without conditions, allowing them the space to be felt, processed, and integrated.

Just as we naturally accept the act of breathing, we must acknowledge and honor our emotions as they surface. When we suppress or ignore them, they build up, eventually intensifying our pain and deepening our misery.

By allowing ourselves to fully experience and release these feelings, we unburden and achieve emotional balance, cultivating a healthy relationship with ourselves and others.

Recognizing and accepting the presence of both positive and negative aspects in relationships leads to more realistic and harmonious interactions.

Navigating conflict in our human connections requires intention, empathy, and emotional awareness. Here's how I attempt to approach it with care and optimism:

Communicate with Vulnerability:

- *Speak Your Truth.* Share your emotions openly without pointing blame. Focus on how you feel, rather than accusing your loved one. This softens the conversation and invites understanding.

- *Listen to Understand.* Allow your loved one to speak without interruption. Listening without bias, meets their need to be valued. By acknowledging their feelings, it shows that you care about their perspective, building a bridge of connection.

Foster Empathy and Understanding:

- *Acknowledge Their Pain.* Even if you don't agree with their point of view, acknowledge the validity of their feelings. This simple act of confirmation meets their need to be seen, diffuses defensiveness and promotes mutual respect.
- *Step Into Their World.* Make a genuine effort to see the conflict through their eyes. Empathy turns confrontation into a shared experience rather than a fight.

Manage Your Emotions:

- *Stay Grounded.* Conflict can stir intense feelings, but reacting impulsively only adds fuel to the fire. If emotions run high, pause, breathe, and take a step back to process and balance, until you can approach the issue calmly.

- *Use Lightness.* When appropriate, a touch of humor can ease the tension and remind you both that you're in this together, not against each other.

Collaborate, Don't Compete:

- *Work as a Team.* Rather than aiming to win the argument, or who's right and wrong, focus on resolving the issue together. View the conflict as an opportunity to grow, finding a solution that benefits both of you. It's ok to agree to disagree.
- *Embrace Flexibility.* Be willing to compromise when needed. Flexibility shows that you value the relationship more than being right, and it fosters a sense of partnership.

Release and Forgive:

- *Let Go of the Past.* Once the conflict is resolved, don't hold onto past grievances. Letting go of old wounds creates space for healing and prevents the buildup of resentment.

Rebuild the Bond:

- *Reconnect with Love.* After the storm, take time to emotionally reconnect. Whether through physical affection, shared laughter, or simply being present with each other, this reinforces your bond and serves as a great reminder of the love and adoration that is mutually shared.

When conflict is approached with vulnerability, empathy, integrity, and a shared desire to grow, it transforms from a place of tension into an opportunity to deepen intimacy, trust, and love.

Advocate for Mental Health

Throughout my career as a public servant, I have witnessed how mental health struggles are often misunderstood, dismissed, or stigmatized, creating what I believe to be the true pandemic of our time.

To inspire healing, we must confront this crisis with honest self-examination, recognizing how deeply our emotional, psychological, and social well-being shapes the way we think, feel, and act.

In my own journey, I have learned that unresolved trauma often manifests as mental health issues, affecting not only our quality of life but also the energy we project into the world. When left unaddressed, these wounds perpetuate the cycle of suffering.

The mental health crisis is very real. It impacts everything, from how we manage stress and make decisions to how we nurture relationships. When we are chronically dysregulated or out of balance, we enter the freeze state. This can lead to anxiety, depression, burn-out, and overwhelming distress that disrupt our very essence, robbing us of joy.

What makes these struggles even more complex is the bias that surrounds this subject matter. Historically, these challenges were seen in society as personal failings or embarrassment, a perceived outlook of humiliation that still lingers today.

Every human being on Earth is battling some form of mental health challenge, and these struggles should never be seen as weaknesses to hide. Viewing them this way only deepens the shame so many already carry.

Growing up, I was taught to bury my pain, to silence my voice and suppress my emotions. This conditioning only reinforced the misconception that mental health issues are less significant than physical ones, when in reality, they are equally vital to our overall well-being.

We are now becoming more aware of invisible disabilities like anxiety, depression, and other mental health conditions. Unlike physical injuries, these struggles don't show visible symptoms, making them harder to diagnose and often minimized.

For example, while a broken bone is treated with urgency, the internal fractures caused by depression or lingering concussion symptoms are frequently overlooked, leaving many to suffer in silence.
Gender and racial biases further complicate the mental health landscape.

Men, often taught to suppress vulnerability, are less likely to seek help, while diverse communities face systemic barriers, mistrust, and cultural stigmas that hinder access to proper care.

As someone who identifies with invisible disabilities and neurodiversity, I have experienced these biases firsthand. Conditions like ADHD, autism, and dyslexia are frequently labeled as "disorders" rather than unique neurological variations. Society tends to stigmatize neurodivergent individuals, overlooking the opportunity to celebrate their strengths.

Many colleagues with ADHD, for example, possess remarkable creativity and innovative thinking but often struggle with traditional time-management structures, leading to frustration. By shifting our perspective and recognizing the unique wiring of their brains, we could create environments that harness their strengths and empower their contributions.

Similarly, I have learned that autistic individuals process sensory input and emotions in distinct ways. Instead of forcing them to conform, embracing their unique perspectives can broaden our understanding of human diversity. Sadly, neurodiversity is still often viewed as something to be "fixed" rather than celebrated as part of the rich spectrum of our civilization.

In my own healing journey, combining medical intervention with therapy and holistic metaphysical principles like the Law of Vibration has been transformative.

This universal principle teaches that everything, including our thoughts and emotions, operates at different frequencies. Understanding this allows us to consciously shift away from suffering programs, empowering us to choose higher states of well-being.

When anxiety heightens due to environmental misalignment, practices like listening to Solfeggio Frequencies, which resonate at specific vibrational rates, can be incredibly soothing.

These frequencies are known to create new neuro pathways in the brain to eliminate emotional blockages. For example, if we are tuned to 741Hz music, it can aid brain cells in forming new connections to achieve balance in our throat center.

The vibrational sounds strengthened by sensory anchors can calm overstimulation, reduce inflammation, and regulate the vagus nerve within the parasympathetic nervous system, offering inner peace, clarity, and focus. This practice not only sharpens mental precision but also restores balance, empowering us to manage anxiety and emotional distress more effectively.

We may also find grounding techniques like deep conscious breathing or time spent in nature helpful for regulating our emotional vibrations. These practices shift our energy emittance from states of anxiety to a place of tranquility.

Even something as simple as practicing gratitude can raise our vibrational frequency. Focusing on strengths rather than shortcomings helps us shift from feelings of inadequacy to empowerment.

I understand that depression can feel like a dense emotional prison, but through practices like meditation or immersing in uplifting creative expressions, we can raise our frequency and break free.

From my perspective, anxiety reveals itself as overwhelming feelings of worry, fear, and apprehension about future events. It often manifests as a pervasive sense of unease, making even simple tasks feel daunting.

Individuals grappling with anxiety may experience irrational and intrusive thoughts, racing hearts, or physical symptoms such as sweating and trembling when confronted by stress.

I have learned through my own experience that this condition can take many forms, from social anxiety disorder, panic attacks, and specific phobias. Anxiety frequently disrupts sleep, causing insomnia or irregular sleep patterns that lead to fatigue and decreased overall well-being.

Furthermore, it activates the body's fight-or-flight response, resulting in increased heart rate, elevated blood pressure, and heightened alertness.

Cognitively, anxiety can impair concentration, memory, and decision-making abilities, making it difficult to function effectively in daily life. The impact is far-reaching, often disrupting daily activities, straining relationships, and diminishing overall quality of life.

For those who struggle with anxiety, the world can feel like an unpredictable storm, leaving them in a constant state of vigilance and distress.

Combined with proper medical care, I have learned to balance my anxiety through mindfulness, soul retrieval, and sound healing. These methods stabilize emotional vibrations, moving us from dread to inner-peace.
The universal laws of energy reminds us that we are not defined by our mental health struggles.

We have the power to consciously shift our internal state, elevating our emotional vibration and transforming how we experience life. Through this awareness, we can heal, grow, and live in alignment with the highest frequencies of joy and harmony.

Examples of Integration

To incorporate some of the philosophical concepts into daily life, consider the following practices:

Path to Divine Essence: Forgiveness is a transformative pathway to reconnect with your divine essence. By practicing forgiveness, you free yourself from the heavy weight of resentment and anger—emotions rooted in the survival-based ego.

This release not only restores your inner power but also aligns you with your true self. As you let go of negativity, you create space for love and compassion to blossom, enriching your life with a sense of purity and connection to your authentic being.

Reconnecting with the Authentic Self: Meditation or quiet contemplation acts as a gateway to your authentic self. With consistent practice, you can subdue the ego's influence, nurturing a profound sense of inner peace and clarity. This mindful journey allows you to rise above the constant chatter of the mind, enabling you to reconnect with the serene essence that resides within you.

Impact of Conscious Reality: Your consciousness and vibrational frequency are pivotal in shaping both your reality and the world around you. By changing your perspective and cultivating a positive, high-frequency mindset, you can manifest your desired outcomes and harmonize with the natural flow of the universe.

This awareness empowers you to craft a life of bliss that truly reflects your highest potential.

Recognizing the Tools for Growth: Recognize that your physical body is merely a tool for learning and growth, not your true self.
This perspective encourages you to detach from physical limitations and prioritize your spiritual evolution. By viewing your body as a sacred vessel for experiences rather than the essence of your being, you can navigate life with greater wisdom and a sense of detachment from the limitations of identity.

Avoiding Labels: Steer clear of judgment, negative gossip, and labeling others, as these behaviors only deepen the chasms of separation and only serves as self-attack. Instead, cultivate empathy and compassion in your interactions. Acknowledge that each person is on their unique *Hero's Odyssey*, navigating their own challenges and triumphs. We are all interconnected with this web of life. Embrace the practice of respectful disagreement, fostering unity and understanding in our diverse journeys.

Focusing on the Present Moment: By anchoring your awareness in the eternal now, you can transcend the false fear-based programs around time, death, and separation. This transformative shift enables you to release attachments and trust the process, allowing you to experience life with profound peace and a deep sense of fulfillment.

Understanding Acceptance: From a metaphysics viewpoint, acceptance is the courageous act of facing reality as it is, without judgment or opposition. It is about surrendering to what is rather than clinging to what should be. Often, we push back against discomfort, thinking that denial or avoidance will shield us from pain. But true growth demands that we lean into that discomfort or anxiety with compassion, allowing ourselves to be vulnerable in the process.

With this approach, we stop fighting against the currents of life and start flowing with it. Instead of reacting impulsively or from a trauma response, we act with clarity, aligning ourselves with deeper wisdom. This shift transforms our relationship with the present moment, releasing the grip of fear and control. In doing so, we unlock the space for healing, integration, and personal evolution.

Metaphysically, acceptance is the gateway to transcending suffering. When we allow emotions and experiences to simply be, without the urge to manipulate them, we free ourselves from the chains of resistance. We stop fixating on outcomes and trust in the Natural Order, understanding that every moment unfolds for our growth.

At its essence, the act of acceptance liberates us. It invites us into a state of flow, where peace replaces struggle, and where we associate with the higher consciousness of our soul. By embracing reality fully, we gain the strength to move forward, transformed, and empowered.

Navigating Resistance

In my experience, resistance is often an unconscious response to challenges, where we instinctively push back against what we find difficult or uncomfortable. However, this defiance can create additional obstacles and prevent us from moving forward.

Resistance shows up in our daily lives in quiet, persistent ways. It's that insistent force that holds us back, keeping us in a cycle of stagnation while we yearn for change or to become better versions of ourselves.

It may begin with procrastination—the silent act of postponing the things we know we should do. We convince ourselves there will be a better time, yet deep down, we know it's a fear of what comes next, or the unknown—a reluctance of what we might uncover if we actually move forward.

Sometimes, it may be more subtle, creeping into our habits. We sabotage our own progress without realizing it. We set goals but undermine them with negative thoughts, unhealthy patterns, or small, seemingly harmless decisions that slowly derail our momentum. There is comfort in staying stuck, because change threatens to expose the vulnerability that we have spent so long protecting.

Then it can show up as perfectionism, the insidious belief that if everything isn't flawless, it is not worth doing. We hide behind this shield, telling ourselves we will change our habit when we are ready, or when the conditions are ideal, full of excuses.

The truth is, we resist stepping into imperfection or shadow integration, where growth truly happens.

Some days, the weight of resistance feels like overwhelm, suffocating us under the sheer magnitude of everything we haven't yet faced. So, we retreat.

We avoid decisions, put off conversations, bury ourselves in distractions, all to escape the discomfort of confronting change.

This may also flare up emotional reactivity. We lash out in frustration, snap at others, or find ourselves irritated at the smallest things. It's not the situation—it is the battle within. The resistance to accept what is, the struggle to control outcomes, to bend the world to our will when we are really just avoiding our own reflection.

At times, it disguises itself as rational. We give ourselves logical reasons for staying where we are—too busy, not the right time, it's not meant to be. But these justifications are just walls we build around our hearts, keeping us from taking the leap we know, deep down, we must take.

Often times, we find ourselves in the comfort zone, the invisible line we draw around ourselves. We stay within its confines because it's familiar and the unknown is daunting. But what we don't realize is that staying in this stagnation is the greatest act of resistance.

Sometimes, the body speaks before the mind can catch up. Resistance manifests as tension, a knot in the stomach, tight shoulders, a pounding headache. Our bodies react to what we are unwilling to face emotionally. The discomfort isn't the external world but the reality we refuse to face.

Blame becomes our escape. We shift responsibility onto others, to circumstances beyond our control. It's easier to believe that the universe has conspired against us than to acknowledge the power we have given away in resisting our own potential.

But when we look closer, resistance is a signal. It's the friction between where we are and where we long to be. And within that tension lies the invitation to break free. To push past worry, perfectionism, the excuses. To step beyond comfort and into the vast space where transformation happens.

From a metaphysical perspective, it may be seen as the ego's effort to maintain control, clinging to familiar patterns that prevent us from evolving. It disrupts the flow of life force energy and inhibits our ability to fully embrace experiences, insights, or changes that would otherwise lead to greater harmony, awareness, and spiritual intelligence.

Releasing resistance allows us to surrender to the Natural Order of the universe, aligning with the flow of universal laws, enabling the creation of new realities and higher levels of consciousness.

Resistance is essentially the tension between the lower aspects of the conditioned mind and the higher, Divine self.

Stop taking things Personally

I have realized that reacting from a place of victimhood often signals a fragile ego hiding beneath insecurities, low self-confidence, and hypercritical trauma response.

Life offers profound opportunities to practice personal mastery by embracing acceptance and emotional regulation, choosing to trust our soul over the egoic projections of others.

It's essential to find balance, recognizing that everyone around us is a teacher—either guiding us to accept, forgive, and let go, or revealing truths that challenge our knowledge and emotional growth, especially when we resist change.

When I find myself in such situations, I remind myself to:

Shift My Perspective: I consider whether someone's comment reflects more on the other person's integration journey than on me. Many people project their own issues, and holding space for them with empathy helps me navigate these interactions.

Practice Self-Compassion: I acknowledge my feelings without dwelling on negative reactions. By healing my need for external validation, I can transmute triggers into opportunities for growth.

Thicken My Skin: Building strong self-worth, inner safety, and trust helps me understand my value and not be swayed by others' opinions.

Communicate Clearly: Instead of assuming negativity, I ask for clarification. Accepting differences is crucial for achieving Oneness. Consciously communicating my needs is a continuous work in progress.

Set Boundaries: I don't play drama games with those who lash out or emit a negative charge. I surround myself with people who accept and understand me. I observe with empathy, not absorb.

Engage in Positive Self-Talk: I challenge negative thoughts with affirmations about my strengths and take feedback constructively, reminding me that all is well.

Let Go of Control: I remember that I can't control others' actions or words, only my reactions. Everyone has their own perspective, as do I.

Use Humor: I learn to laugh things off when appropriate, finding lightness in challenging situations.

Discern: I separate my reality from interpretations and false narratives, relying on my intuitive guidance system to seek clarity and understanding.

Acting with Compassion

Living from a place of high-functioning compassion involves transforming the way we respond to others' emotions. Instead of feeling triggered or overwhelmed, we can uplift and empower our interactions. Here's how I have learned to navigate this process:

Focus on Uplifting Experiences: Shift your attention from negative emotions to optimistic, empowering moments. This conscious redirection helps you maintain your alignment, enabling you to offer genuine support without feeling drained.

Embrace Collective Human Potential: Acknowledge the inherent possibility within every individual and the collective. By looking beyond immediate challenges, you open yourself to higher frequencies of connection and action, fostering vital relationships and a sense of community.

Align with Your Higher Self: Connect with your deepest essence, the representative of Divine Infinite Intelligence, by activating your pineal gland. Disconnecting from technology and spending time in nature or practicing quiet contemplation can guide your interactions.

This alignment allows you to rise above draining patterns and approach others from a place of authenticity, knowing, wisdom, and strength.

Your higher self is the truest aspect of your being, transcending the limitations of the ego and physical body.

It is your soul's essence that is linked to the quantum field and the Source of eternal light, holding the knowledge of your true purpose and spiritual evolution.

Unlike the ego, which focuses on survival and external validation, the higher self-embodies devotion, unity, and harmony. It sees the bigger picture, understanding life's challenges and relationships from a more enlightened perspective.

While the ego is driven by lack, desires, and attachments, the higher self is grounded in compassion and trust, recognizing that everything unfolds for your growth and highest potential.

When we tune into this inner voice of wisdom and intuition, we can navigate life with certainty.

From a metaphysical standpoint, the higher self serves as a bridge between our physical experiences and the Divine, guiding us toward self-actualization and inner peace.

By embracing this connection, we can enhance our capacity for compassion and foster deeper, more meaningful relationships.

Stepping into Flow State

From a metaphysical perspective, the flow state is that magical moment when everything just clicks. Imagine you're immersed in something you love—like painting, playing music, writing poetry, or even playing your favorite sport.

Time seems to vanish, and you're completely submerged in the activity. You feel energized, focused, and fully alive, as if the world outside fades away.

In this state, your mind, body, and spirit work together effortlessly. You lose track of time, your thoughts become clear, and challenges feel manageable. It's that sweet spot where your passions meet the task at hand, and every action flows seamlessly, like a river carving through the landscape.

Achieving flow can happen during any activity that engages you deeply. Whether it's running, knitting, or solving a puzzle, the key is finding something that challenges you just enough to keep you on your toes but isn't so difficult that it feels overwhelming.

When you're in flow, you feel a sense of joy and fulfillment, as if you're exactly where you're meant to be. It's a powerful reminder of what it feels like to be truly present, connected to your creative expressions, and alive in the moment.

We step into a state of flow, where life feels more harmonious, and we begin to live in alignment with our true nature. We can do this when we:

Apply Alchemical Principles: Utilize the principles of alchemy to transform unresolved issues, such as soul contracts, family karma, and ancestral wounds. By working through these layers, you enhance your ability to connect deeply and authentically.

Prioritize Self-Care: Consistently nurture yourself with acts of self-love to preserve emotional and energetic harmony. By doing so, you safeguard your well-being, ensuring you can show up for others without draining your own reserves.

Establish Strong Boundaries: Protect your energy by setting firm, clear boundaries, allowing you to stay open to genuine connection while preventing emotional burnout.

Evaluate Connections: Take time to reflect on your relationships, making sure they are rooted in mutual respect and integrity. Avoid relations driven by unresolved trauma or ego-based attachments, choosing instead those that foster growth and understanding.

Resolve Issues: Experiencing disputes are a natural part of any relationship, and disagreements or hurt feelings are inevitable. What sets healthy relationships apart is how we handle those moments—through constructive communication, honesty, mutual regard, and the ability to reconnect after resolving issues.

Relying only on love and reassurance, or avoiding difficult conversations, can actually undermine a relationship. Instead, incorporating humor, knowing when to let things go, and embracing open dialogue are vital to maintaining a strong, loving connection.

When we approach conflicts with compassion, courage, and openness, we not only resolve differences but also deepen our understanding and intimacy, ultimately strengthening the bond we share with our loved ones.

The Power of Ho'oponopono

When I first encountered the powerful prayer of the Hopi people, it felt like stepping into a new world of healing and connection. I learned that this ancient Hawaiian practice goes beyond just reciting a prayer—it's a deep, transformative process of making things right in my relationships with others, the earth, and most importantly, with myself.

The essence of this sacred prayer is rooted in unity and responsibility. It taught me that we are all interconnected, and the experiences I face as an adult are reflections of my own inner state.

By embracing this concept, I began to understand that even when someone hurts me, I still have a part in how I respond and heal.

The core of Ho'oponopono lies in four simple but profound phrases: "I am sorry, Please forgive me, Thank you, and I love you." These words aren't just empty statements—they embody a deep process of repentance, forgiveness, gratitude, and love.

At first, I resisted the idea of taking responsibility for the harm imposed on me in my life. It felt uncomfortable to say sorry to the universe when I wasn't sure what exactly I had done wrong.

But as I continued the mantra, I realized that acknowledging my part in conflicts and seeking forgiveness was more about healing myself than about pointing fingers.

Repeating these phrases became a daily practice for me. Whenever I faced a challenge or felt overwhelmed, I would quietly recite the powerful prayer. The act of expressing gratitude and affirming helped shift my perspective.

I noticed that as I embraced these principles, I felt a profound sense of peace and clarity. Handling conflicts with others became more manageable. Instead of reacting with anger or resentment, I cited this prayer to address the situation from a place of love and accountability.

It wasn't always easy, but the process helped me release old wounds and foster healing in my relationships. It also extended to my own inner work. I found that it helped me confront and heal anger and resentment from past traumas.

It was about acknowledging and forgiving my own self-worth struggles or guilt and then moving forward with a renewed sense of self-love and connection to my inner divinity. I faced resistance at the beginning, and it felt challenging to authentically embrace the practice.

But with time, it became easier and more natural. If I step on a spider, or swaddle a small fruit fly, I automatically go into this prayer of reconciliation. I noticed shifts in my emotional state, a deeper sense of peace, and a greater capacity to love without judgement.

Ho'oponopono has become a significant part of my life, helping me integrate forgiveness and compassion into my daily experiences. It's not just a practice in my toolkit but a way of living that fosters harmony and healing, both within myself and in my interactions with the world around me.

EXPLORING THE ART OF ALCHEMY

As we reach the pinnacle of this journey toward self-mastery, I invite you to delve deeper into the essence of core fundamental concepts. In doing so, we can uncover their intimate connection with the ancient art of alchemy—a process that changes not only the mind but the very essence of our being.

Spiritual alchemy is a sacred journey of transformation, where the base elements of our lower nature—fear, doubt, and ego—are transmuted into the radiant light of higher consciousness and divine wisdom.

This path invites us to refine our being, shedding layers of negativity and illusion that obscure our truest essence. Much like ancient alchemists sought to turn lead into gold, this inner alchemy calls us to elevate our spirit, master the art of inner revolution, and ascend to our most enlightened form.

Through this alchemical process of inner purification, we awaken to the truth that within each of us rests the potential for divine enlightenment and unity with the highest realms of existence.

The transformation begins with dismantling the judgment, discord, and inauthenticity that leave us fragmented. This journey, often turbulent, demands that we confront pain, navigate disunity, and face the shadows that linger within ourselves and the world around us.

It calls for courage, for alchemy requires that we uncover the hidden parts of our soul—the aspects we have long avoided—and embrace them with compassion. In doing so, we reconnect with our innate wholeness.

Each of us bears the sacred responsibility to merge with our inner self, harmonizing the divine feminine and masculine energies through self-reflection, acceptance, and transcendence. *To alchemize what limits us, we must first truly know ourselves.*

As we engage in this inner work, transmuting conflict into peace, we come to view every challenge as an invitation to reconnect with our essence—embracing love and illuminating the parts of us that seek healing. Through this reconnection, we reclaim our divine nature and embody the highest expression of our true selves.

This restoration of personal sovereignty sparks the blossoming of our authentic essence. By breaking free from the unconscious suffering imposed by conditioned beliefs, we activate the alchemy within our *Coherent Heart,* bringing clarity to our vision and revealing the inner radiance that has always existed.

In my journey through alchemy and integration, I discovered the profound symbolism embedded in this ancient practice.
The symbolisms offer deep insights into the expansion of consciousness, guiding us through the inner realms and reminding us that the process of transformation is ultimately a return to our divine origins.

Stages of Growth

From my understanding, Earth, Air, Fire, and Water represent not only physical properties but also different aspects of our human experience:

- Earth: Grounding, stability, the physical body.
- Air: Thought, intellect, and communication.
- Fire: Transformation, passion, and purification.
- Water: Emotions, intuition, and the subconscious mind.

They are a metaphor for our inner process to realizing self-mastery. It is the unification of opposites—masculine and feminine energies, or the conscious and unconscious mind.

This process unfolds in seven distinct stages of personal growth in our efforts to attain spiritual intelligence:

Calcination: This first stage involves breaking down the survival-based ego. This happens when we confront the false identities and narratives we have constructed around fear, control, and attachment—burning away the false masks that no longer serve us.

Dissolution: In this stage, we release the emotional baggage that has weighed us down, dissolving past trauma patterns, unresolved feelings, and limiting beliefs. They flow away like water, liberating the heart and mind.

Discernment: Once we release and unblock our lower energy centers, we begin to identify the pure and impure aspects of ourselves. This stage is about developing our ability to discern truth from false narratives—unraveling what is essential to our growth from what hinders us, bringing clarity to our inner landscape.

Conjunction: In this consolidative stage, we unite the conscious and unconscious mind. By merging logic with intuition, light with shadow, we achieve balance and harmony, creating a unified whole where our inner and outer worlds align.

Fermentation: This stage marks spiritual awakening and rebirth where our spirit begins to rise, nurtured by the wisdom we have cultivated in our *Coherent Heart.* Like new life emerging from decay, our soul awakens to deeper insights, bridging the lower aspects with the higher intelligence and aligning with our higher self.

Distillation: Finally, we refine the soul, stripping away any lingering impurities. Through this process, we reach higher states of awareness, achieving clarity, insight, self-mastery, and enlightenment, where the essence of who we are is fully revealed

Coagulation: Attaining spiritual wisdom and embodying enlightenment or the Christ consciousness archetype.

These stages mirror the path of spiritual alchemy, where our soul is transformed from base existence to radiant consciousness, awakening to the divine potential within. With purification and inner balance, we can achieve unity with the one Infinite Intelligence of Source consciousness.

In the realm of esoteric teachings, alchemical symbols like the square, triangle, and circle carry profound ancient meanings, which also reflects the stages of our human evolution.

The **square** represents the material world, the tangible realm of form and structure where we begin our journey. Rooted in the four elements—earth, air, fire, and water—it symbolizes the foundation of our existence, a world bound by the limitations of ego and the physical plane.

Here, we experience life's challenges, where stability often becomes confinement, and the call of awakening stirs within us.

The **triangle** emerges as a symbol of aspiration and change. With its three points, it reflects the union of body, mind, and spirit, guiding us toward spiritual ascent. It is the alchemical fire that urges us to rise beyond the confines of the square, seeking balance and harmony within. As we confront the shadows of our inner world, the triangle becomes the path that points us toward higher consciousness, challenging us to transcend fear and limitation.

Finally, the **circle** embodies unity, wholeness, and infinity. It transcends the square's boundaries and the triangle's desires, representing the soul's return to our divine essence.

The circle speaks of eternity—of cycles that never truly end but flow seamlessly into one another. It is the symbol of enlightenment, where duality dissolves, and the Oneness of all things is revealed.

Just like the ancient structures of the Great Pyramid of Giza, these symbols map the alchemical journey of transformation: from the material and ego-bound world of the square, through the fire of the triangle's ascension, to the infinite unity of the circle, where we reclaim our divine nature.

This convergence represents the unity of body, mind, and spirit, reflecting the alchemist's journey toward achieving wholeness.

Together, they illustrate how divine energy flows through the laws of rhythm, polarity, and karma, revealing that enlightenment comes through embracing the totality of our being, both shadow and light.

They remind us of the ongoing interplay between the seen and unseen worlds, inviting us to balance and harmonize our own internal dualities. They guide us from a fragmented sense of self in suffering toward harmonious unity with the Divine.

Each symbol is a diagram for navigating the physical and spiritual planes, helping us elevate our consciousness.

Dissolving the division between our inner and outer worlds is essential for spiritual growth. Every moment—whether joyful or challenging—offers a valuable lesson, urging us to raise our consciousness.

When we move beyond survival mode and harmonize our nervous system, we start to see how our thoughts and projections actively shape our reality.
Confronting blind spots like pride, anxiety, and judgment becomes pivotal in this process. By embracing this inner work, we begin to balance the dualities within ourselves,

leading to deeper self-awareness and a profound sense of unity.

The Nature of Light and Shadow Integration

Embarking on the path of self-realization has been nothing short of transformative. It cracked open my heart, forcing me to confront the parts of myself I once avoided. It wasn't easy but I learned to stop evading my inner child and quit pouring energy into draining situations.

This journey revealed the importance of safeguarding my inner peace and recognizing my inherent worth. By shedding people-pleasing patterns and limiting beliefs about my self-worth, I embraced my vulnerability. I found the courage and strength to rise and to integrate my shadow aspects with kindness rather than judgment.

Through the power of self-love, I released outdated views and paradigms, discovering that the most vital relationship I have is with my limitless self. This ongoing evolution of growth and self-discovery is nurtured by authenticity and self-acceptance, reminding me that accepting my divine essence and recognizing my true value is the foundation of this journey.

Years ago, on my first trip to Italy, I was initiated into the dark night, a catalyst that launched me on my *Hero's*

Odyssey. It was a profound confrontation with my own fears, teaching me that shadows are simply light obstructed—darkness existing only in the absence of illumination.

But I have come to understand that light itself never depends on shadows to exist. As a force of electromagnetic radiation, light shines independently, revealing the world in all its clarity.

We, too, are fractals of that light, emanating from Source consciousness, carrying the potential to illuminate the darkest corners of our being.

From a scientific perspective, I realized that darkness occurs when light is absorbed or fails to reach an area. It's an intriguing interplay between light and matter—between visibility and obscurity. When light meets an object, it's either absorbed, reflected, or transmitted.

Dark objects, like a black surface, absorb nearly all light, leaving little to reflect back, creating the sensation of deep shadow. This process even generates heat, which intensifies the contrast between light and shadow.

This perspective has helped me to understand the ongoing cosmic dance between light and darkness—which extends beyond physics, hinting at deeper truths about the nature of our reality. It touches on the mysteries of black holes, where even light cannot escape, reminding us that darkness, too, plays a vital role in shaping the universe.

And so, I have learned to not fear the negatively polarized aspects of shadow, but to see it as part of the whole—a balance, where light remains the guiding force that leads us back to ourselves.

In the grand tapestry of the universe, this concept resonates deeply. *Darkness, then, is a dynamic force—a catalyst shaped by the energy of light, inviting us to explore the depths of what lies beyond our sight.*

Honesty and Self-Reflection

Being truthful with ourselves can be one of the most difficult challenges we face. I have found that engaging in deep self-reflection and examining my state of being creates a sacred space to contemplate integrity in its rawest form.

The daily acceptance of my inner child, especially through the green ray portal of my heart, has become a powerful measure of my growth and expansion. This unwavering devotion serves as a profound indicator of my embodiment, reflecting how deeply I have aligned with my true essence.

For me, enlightenment isn't about uncovering objective truths but about reconnecting with my pure essence. It's an alchemical process of remembering who I truly am and aligning with my fundamental nature.

This insight also reveals that the universe doesn't shield us from discomfort but supports us in co-creating experiences that cultivate both safety and vulnerability.

By transcending fears, doubts, and skepticism, I approach each day with wonder and receptiveness, allowing for growth and transformation.

Electromagnetic Field

Joy exemplifies the essence of our existence, a force that connects us through the loving energy we emit.
When I open my heart to the positive charge of love, bliss, or eternal joy, the vibration within my heart's electromagnetic field expands outward by six feet, influencing my well-being and creating an invisible connection with the world around me.

I have also learned to achieve bliss consciousness, embracing life with boundless openness. These feelings of paradise are not shaped by external events but nurtured through meditation, mindfulness, and deep inner contemplation.

In this elevated awareness, I realize that joy and peace aren't something we need to seek—they already reside within us, waiting to be unlocked by shedding the layers of ego, fear, and doubt. It's a complete awakening, a harmonious alignment with the Divine flow of the universe, where fulfillment naturally radiates from the core of our being.

Inner Abundance

I realize that true wealth emerges from a mindset grounded in trust, an awareness of a higher purpose, and a harmonious flow of universal energy.
It transcends external possessions and fleeting fame, which often fail to deliver inner peace or spiritual richness. Instead, real abundance is cultivated through gratitude, love, kindness, and acceptance, nurturing a genuine sense of fulfillment.

Real abundance is an expression of our inner state, deeply rooted in the flow of universal energy. To embody this state of being, we must first align ourselves with the vibration of gratitude, self-worth, and value, recognizing that abundance is not something we chase but something we already are.

Esoteric wisdom teaches that the universe is a vast web of interconnected energy, and when we acknowledge our place within it, we tap into an infinite source of wealth.

The belief in scarcity is an illusion that keeps us disconnected from this natural flow. Shifting our mindset from lack to appreciation invites more inner abundance into our lives, as energy responds to our thoughts and emotions.

We are co-creators of our reality, and by intentionally focusing on what we want to manifest from our *Coherent Heart*, we align ourselves with the outcomes we desire.

This elevated energy follows when we live in harmony with our purpose and act in alignment with our highest self. It's about trusting that the universe provides what we need in divine timing and embracing the process without fear.

Generosity is a vital part of this flow. The more we give—whether it's love, time, creativity, or resources—the more we create space for receiving. But this cycle also requires that we open ourselves to accepting the blessings meant for us, knowing we are worthy.

However, we must first confront the limiting beliefs that block abundance. Through deep inner alchemy, we release the subconscious patterns of unworthiness, fear, or scarcity that hold us back.

By clearing these energetic blockages, we allow abundance to flow freely, transforming our lives.

This practice begins by recognizing our intrinsic worth and nurturing it through daily acts of self-love. Affirmations like "I AM deserving of magic and bliss" and "Thank you Universe for all the beauty and abundance that is within me and around me".

When we align to our higher self and reshape our mindset, we break down limiting beliefs of the subconscious mind and welcome prosperity and fulfillment. We begin to naturally attract what resonates with our elevated vibration and sense of self.

The key is to stay fully present. Abundance is often missed when we focus on past regrets or future worries. By practicing mindfulness, we can attune to the richness of each moment, appreciating the beauty and opportunities that surround us.

Through deep contemplation, breathwork, or grounding exercises, we can clear fear, negativity, and self-doubt, allowing a free flow of energy that supports our inner growth. When we visualize ourselves thriving, joyful, and at peace, we allow the vision to inspire our actions.

Spiritual wealth is not simply what we accumulate; it's a reflection of the joy, fulfillment, harmony, and connection we experience and emit.

As we live in alignment with our purpose and knowing, this prosperity of beauty and magic becomes a natural consequence, revealing itself in countless forms.

It serves as a daily reminder that we are always supported, loved, and always enough.

Redefining Vulnerability

Over the years, I have come to realize that vulnerability is often mistaken for weakness, seen as an exposure to uncertainty and potential danger. However, when we embrace this concept, it becomes a powerful act of authenticity. It allows us to present our genuine selves to the world without apology.

This requires a willingness and ability to openly express our feelings, thoughts, and experiences without causing harm to another, even when they might be uncomfortable. It involves a level of honesty that allows us to connect deeply with others.

For example, in Part 2 of this book, I open up about my own journey through menopause—a poetic expression marked by vulnerability and self-discovery. Letting down my guard and truly feeling into my body revealed the profound ways estrogen deficiency was affecting my physical health and vitality.

The stigma and silence around this natural phase of life can feel suffocating, which is why it's so important to break the taboo and normalize conversations about the hormonal changes every woman will face.

Although menopause is inevitable, we don't have to suffer through the change in silence. From the unsettling shifts in appearance to the exhaustion of sleepless nights, to the neurological, psychological, and sexual challenges—it's time that medical professionals provide women with real, science-backed solutions for managing these changes.

Raising awareness and offering practical tools to address the natural decline in estrogen is key to preventing serious health risks like diabetes, dementia, osteoporosis, heart disease, high cholesterol, and excess weight gain around the belly.

By empowering women to take charge of their bodies and their health, we ensure that this transition, though challenging, becomes a passage in our *Hero's Odyssey* to greater strength, confidence, and self-care

I have learned that vulnerability requires us to dismantle the defensive walls we build—personal coping mechanisms, deceit, delusion, and the masks we wear to shield our inner child from the pain of social rejection. These protective shields were created to maintain our comfort, but they often isolate us from deeper connections.

At its core, we learn to feel and understand our emotions on a profound level. This involves honoring the sacred feelings that shape our individuality, acknowledging the parts of ourselves that have endured judgment and rejection.

It calls for the expression and processing of negative emotions with self-compassion, dissolving self-denial and embracing truth with dignity.

To be vulnerable is to accept discomfort and allow healing to unfold in its many forms, with courage as the guiding force in our lives.

Pure love possesses the remarkable ability to dissolve fear of hurt and judgment. When we remove these barriers, resistance to vulnerability diminishes.

By allowing our hearts to embrace this concept, we forge deeper connections with ourselves and others, creating a safe space for transformative growth.

Fulfillment of Fundamental Needs

Emotions are natural and essential aspects of our being, offering valuable insights into our inner states. They act as a feedback loop, signaling whether our personal needs are being met and guiding us towards necessary actions.

Theories such as "**Maslow's Hierarchy of Needs and the Self-Determination Theory**" reveal that our sense of well-being is intricately linked to how well our core needs are met, especially those established in early childhood, before the age of seven.

These fundamental needs—security, love, belonging, and self-worth—form the foundation of our emotional and psychological well-being. Understanding this connection unlocked profound life lessons for me, revealing not only how deeply these needs influence our sense of fulfillment but also how they drive our personal growth and ability to live with purpose and resilience.

Over the past year, I have navigated profound changes that have reshaped my life. Confronting deep-seated abandonment issues opened a pathway to understanding my true yearning: the need for physical connection.

Touch, a hug, the warmth of companionship—these became essential elements of my integration journey.

This longing found its manifestation in the caring of an adorable fur baby. The innocent spirit allows the vastness of love residing in my heart to flow freely into another being. Each gentle cuddle, every shared moment of fun and joy, becomes a balm for my soul, filling the void that had lingered.

In this relationship, I also found an opportunity to transcend co-dependent patterns. I learned to give and receive love without losing myself in the process, embracing a healthier dynamic that honored both my needs and those of my furry companion.

This journey has not only deepened my capacity for love but also fortified my spirit, allowing me to reclaim my sense of self while fostering a bond that is pure and transformative.

I have realized that animals are inherently connected to the Natural Order, serving as reminders of the grounding and healing forces that exist in the natural world. Their presence evokes a sense of peace, drawing us into the present moment and inviting us to reconnect with the earth beneath our feet.

In their innocence, animals embody the rhythms of nature—whether it's the way a dog eagerly embraces the sun or how a cat finds solace in a quiet corner. They teach us to slow down, to breathe, and to appreciate the beauty surrounding us.

Their instinctual understanding of the environment encourages us to tune in to the sights, sounds, and sensations that often go unnoticed in our busy lives.

The healing power of animals is undeniable. Interactions with them can reduce stress and anxiety, lower blood pressure, and elevate our mood. Their unconditional love offers refuge, reminding us of the principle of giving and receiving.

When we engage with animals with kindness and devotion, we often find ourselves enveloped in a sense of safety and belonging—a prompt of the nurturing energy that the universe provides.

In times of struggle, the companionship of an animal can be transformative. They ground us in the present, encouraging us to release worries and embrace the simple joys of life.

Their playful spirits inspire us to reconnect with our own inner child, fostering a sense of wonder and gratitude.

By forging a bond with animals, we not only nurture our own well-being but also deepen our connection to nature itself. This relationship becomes a source of strength, healing, and joy, reminding us of the profound interconnectedness of all living beings. In their presence, we find the grace to embody the devotion of love consciousness that exists within us.

Through this experience, I have learned that the healthy relationships we cultivate, whether with other humans or animals, can heal the deepest wounds and guide us toward our path to wholeness. My fur baby has become a cherished companion, fulfilling my need to feel connected. This sense of belonging fosters emotional security.

Having a healthy co-regulation process allows for deep connection without creating reliance. It's about thriving together while remaining strong individually. I have also found that isolation or feelings of rejection often hide a deeper longing for love, leading to people-pleasing or seeking approval from others. The solution is to recognize and affirm our own truth, standing confidently in our authenticity.

Fear of change can leave us stuck, paralyzed by the desire for stability. But when we release our need to control outcomes and embrace life's natural ebb and flow, we break free from stagnation. We uplevel and step into growth, learning to move with the currents of change instead of resisting them.

Loneliness, when misunderstood, can push us into empty relationships just to avoid our solitary. The real answer is learning to cherish our own presence, which opens the door to meaningful, fulfilling connections that truly resonate on a deeper level.

By recognizing these emotional patterns and addressing their core needs, we unlock the potential for deep personal transformation. Through self-compassion and conscious effort, we learn to appreciate our emotions, creating a life that feels balanced, authentic, and genuinely fulfilling.

"In the depth of winter, I finally learned that within me, there lay an invincible summer."— Albert Camus

Transcendence and Choice

In this realm of density, suffering touches us all, but we face a choice: hold onto it as a shield or embrace the lessons it offers and find healing.

I have come to understand that paradise, or the concept of a new earth, isn't a distant destination—it's a state of consciousness. It's the realm of a heightened vibration where integrity, balance, and harmony converge within my perception.

This is where the divine feminine energy flows through me, grounding me in truth and integrity. As I walk fearlessly through the fires of renewal, I unite with the divine masculine—the warrior spirit—illuminating my path with grace and harmony.

Within my heart field, I carry sacred codes of abundance and authentic expression. My journey through this timeline is a process of alchemically transmuting the burdens of conditioning and suffering. By embracing my own transformative process, I turn pain into power.

Guided by intuition and inner knowing, I rely on the light within rather than external forces. The green ray of my heart serves as a compass, leading me toward personal sovereignty and true freedom.

My third eye, the pineal gland, connects me to unseen realms and dimensions, aligning my consciousness with the universe. As I unite with my higher self through meditation and reflection, I access and live from the heart space which is essential to my evolution.

Achieving coherence between the heart and mind opens the door to infinite wisdom, allowing me to learn from life's lessons with clarity and peace. I realize that while my human mind is rooted in duality, prone to worry and fear, my spirit is anchored in the Law of Oneness, guided by the power of love.

When I encounter scarcity, doubt, or uncertainty, I turn inward, revisiting cherished memories of joy and harmony to remind my mind of the truths held by my heart.

Over time, my mind has learned to align with these philosophies, finding solace in the joy that naturally flows from within.

In my integration journey, facing unprocessed and negatively charged emotions has been a profound experience.

Instead of resisting them, I now see them as messengers of truth, pointing out areas that may require additional integration. Through this acceptance, I have discovered a deeper sense of peace and growth.

For example, I have come to realize that feelings of sadness may point to perceived lack, anger reveals excessive attachment, and fear indicates an attempt to control. By understanding these emotions, I can transform them into sources of positively charged feelings, finding wisdom in the process.

In the dream of eternal consciousness, I find myself engaged in the journey of discovering the dreamer while embracing my human form. I have partnered up with my ego, yet my spirit holds the celestial essence of all that is, with the freedom to actualize my divine potential within my human conduit.

In my physical form, I experience the world through color, motion, sound, and touch, all of which are subtle energies that harmonize to bring healing and coherence to my mind, body, and spirit.

My body is a sensitive receptor of electromagnetic energy, perceiving it as color, and I hear compression airwaves as sound. My skin, too, senses and transmits signals to my brain, connecting me to the frequencies around me.

Sound, color, and all aspects of energy echo with one another, and this resonance, especially in higher harmonics, raises vibrations not just in me, but in my environment, animals and plants as well.

Shapes, numbers, geometric designs, and motions all contribute to this vibrational harmony. By focusing on clearing my biofield and releasing energetic blockages, I can achieve a state of balance. (Source: "The Science of BioGeometry", The Journal of Natural and Social Philosophy, 2015 by Jerry Gin Ph.D.)

Instead of the outdated spiritual practice of discarding or "killing" my human ego persona, I have come to understand that the ***Hero's Odyssey* is a journey of integration, not rejection**. It's about celebrating the full spectrum of individuated path, including our shadow—the dark aspects we often avoid. By becoming aware of these parts of myself, I stopped judging my trauma, recognizing that repressing it only makes it my reality.

Through this bold acceptance, when we stop judging ourselves, we naturally stop judging others.

I now see my human experience as an essential part in the web of existence. Just as every ray of sunlight is intricately linked to the grand sun, I too am a ray of light emanating from the universal mind—the Infinite Intelligence.

By embracing my human form, I reconnect with the eternal life force energy of love consciousness that resides within the quantum field of Oneness. This profound connection unveils the essence of my true nature, revealing that I am neither finite nor separate from Source.

Embodiment and Wisdom

It is my view that the highest law of the universe is balance. Everything exists in a state of vibration, where positive and negative polarities continuously flow in a rhythmic dance.

Every action, thought, and emotion sets off an energetic ripple, triggering a subtle yet equal reaction. This dynamic interchange of contrasts—between what we want and what we resist—drives expansion and growth. Living harmoniously means embracing the flow of both giving and receiving, aligning ourselves with the natural coherence of the universe.

In contrast, my ego, conditioned by fear and scarcity, often defaults to taking, holding, and controlling. This disrupts the law of balance, creating negative karmic imprints and a sense of disharmony. Understanding this, I strive to align my actions with the universal rhythm of reciprocity, maintaining equilibrium within myself and the world around me.

When we live in harmony, we are the embodiment of love—a powerful force that carries us through the chaotic yet beautiful journey of human life. As seekers of truth, we venture through the delicate terrain of relationships, uncovering the profound mystical mysteries of existence.

My transformation is a continuous, evolving journey. Primarily, it entails transcending the illusion of separation from Source, releasing fear, and facing the darkness that once held power over me.

On this path, I have also learned the art of aloneness—finding peace in solitude and connecting with the rhythmic beats of my heart field. This inner chamber is where pure love resides, a sacred crystalline space within that reflects the divine essence we all carry.

The ability to embrace solitude measures how close I am to my divine nature. By recognizing this reality, I have cultivated a deep, unconditional devotion to all things, including myself. This journey has removed the need for external validation, allowing me to fill any inner void with the richness of my soul.

The depth of my inner world strengthens my capacity to love without limits. My ability to hold higher frequencies of light depends on how deeply I confront the shadows. As the world is set ablaze in the fires of collective transmutation, we stand at the edge of an intense alchemy of the soul.

Love, for me, is the essence of unity. But to truly connect with others, I must first find that unity within—the raw, undeniable truth born from accepting every part of myself. The *Hero's Odyssey* has led me to confront and dissolve every barrier to love. By embracing all aspects of my humanness, I clear the way to embody bliss consciousness, where harmony flows effortlessly and abundantly.

Just as ancient alchemists aimed to turn lead into gold, *the spiritual journey is about transforming our shadow aspects into light.*

However, being human means that sometimes we fall back into old, outdated patterns. If I find myself complaining, blaming, or making excuses, I realize I am not stepping into the person I want to embody.

Negative reactions, whether warranted or not, only harm me. It's akin to drinking poison in hopes that someone else will suffer from it. These fleeting emotional responses anchor my body and mind to the past, allowing stress hormones to wreak havoc and create dis-ease.

Each moment spent in that cycle only prolongs my suffering, holding me hostage to memories that no longer serve me. It's time to free ourselves from this self-inflicted pain and choose a path toward healing and liberation.

The key to breaking free from old patterns rests in embracing the present moment. When I let go of expectations tied to an anticipated future or the comfort of a familiar past, I enter the space where true transformation begins.

Beyond the constraints of my former self, I shift from the rigid boundaries of physical reality into a fluid, quantum existence. By aligning a focused mind with clear intention and heightened emotions, I generate a powerful magnetic field through my heart's energy.

This connection to the quantum field creates a signature that bridges my thoughts to the reality I wish to manifest. The more deeply I align with this field, the faster my intentions take form. From this space of harmony, creativity flows effortlessly, no longer bound by struggle or effort.

As the architect of my life, I recognize that to transcend betrayal or pain, I must cultivate emotions more powerful than the wounds or trauma I have endured. My devotion to this practice anchors me in the present, where healing and synchronicity naturally unfold.

When my thoughts are disordered, my nervous system reflects this, affecting my well-being. Achieving balance requires restoring rhythm to both my mind and body. By shifting my brainwaves, I invite harmony back into my being, signaling every cell to heal.

In this state of heart-mind coherence, my spiritual intelligence activates, allowing my body to restore itself. During deep relaxation, especially in the theta brainwave state, I access a realm where my mind can be rewired, empowering transformation and reshaping my reality.

I AM the co-creator of my life, fully capable of transcending limitations and embracing the endless possibilities in the now moment. Through inner alchemy, I harness the elements of earth, water, air, and fire to purify and elevate myself, refining my inner world to achieve self-actualization.

The *Hero's Odyssey* begins by facing the ego, confronting the shadow, and releasing attachments. This path of deep reflection clears limiting beliefs, followed by purification and spiritual rebirth. As the true self emerges, clarity brings peace and self-mastery.

When we retrieve the lost aspects of our soul and integrate elevated wisdom, we align with the golden light of the Logos, embodying love consciousness and stepping fully into our sovereign power.

Final Reflections

If we view the yin and yang spheres as a framework for creation, being, and the balance of opposites, we see that these polarities are complementary aspects of a greater whole.

Each element, except for disorder and entropy, contributes to the energy hierarchy that makes up the Universe. Even chaos can be a catalyst for creating more structure in the Natural Order, depending on how we respond to challenges in each present moment.

If everything is part of a coherent system of life, then all things contribute to our evolution and the Divine Order. Often, we resist or devalue the things we dislike or wish to avoid—those elements linger in the shadows of our collective consciousness.

But this resistance or insistence of our rigid beliefs reflects our reluctance to learn from polarity, which shows us where we need to organize our reality. When we feel disconnected or incomplete, we are attached to the illusion of disorder. Instead of integrating opposing elements, we blame ourselves, believing we have somehow attracted negative karma.

In today's world, attention is our most valuable resource, and inorganic algorithms are designed to capture it. While they play a significant role in shaping our interactions with the world, the most powerful algorithm isn't found in technology—it's the one we create within our own quantum field of intelligence.

When we learn to transmute suffering into purpose, our perspective on life transforms profoundly. The process of softening allows us to shift our outlook dramatically. True power emerges when we close off negative energetic patterns. The most effective way to end these cycles is not to react but to starve them—refusing to return negativity or feed its charge.
By consciously withdrawing our focus from what drains or hinders us, we can redirect that energy toward new goals, passions, and opportunities, creating space for growth to flourish. Letting go becomes a gentle shift in focus toward what truly matters, enabling positive change to unfold organically. In this way, we foster new organic algorithms for living, where joy and fulfillment can thrive, guiding us toward a brighter, more purposeful existence.

Each time we hand over our decision-making to external systems, we sacrifice aspects of ourselves—our focus, energy, and identity—allowing technology to dictate where we invest our awareness. But the feedback loop that truly matters is the one inside us.

This internal loop, our consciousness, weaves thoughts into emotions and emotions into impulses, ultimately guiding our decisions and shaping our reality. When we find ourselves repeating the same patterns—meeting similar people, making familiar mistakes, or facing recurring challenges—our consciousness is signaling an unlearned lesson, urging us to evolve.

Life's repeated themes are not random; they are reflections of our unresolved experiences, meant to prompt growth.

When these patterns persist, it's because we haven't yet embraced the opportunity for transformation. The soul's organic feedback loop of consciousness will continue reflecting these lessons until we confront them. It's not about avoiding these cycles, but about recognizing them as the foundation for our evolution.

Only by taking ownership of this internal algorithm—our attention and awareness—can we break free and consciously shape the collective reality we desire.

While external algorithms anticipate our behavior by feeding us curated content, they operate on the assumption that we are static, driven by subconscious habits. These systems dominate our digital experiences, relying on past data to predict future actions. This confinement to predictable patterns traps us in cycles that reinforce outdated beliefs, hindering our capacity for genuine growth and the development of spiritual intelligence.

To break free, we must consciously challenge these confines, embracing our dynamic nature and seeking experiences that expand our understanding and awareness.

There are two paths to understanding consciousness: inorganic, driven by machine learning, and the organic, rooted in our genetic blueprint, higher awareness, and free will. The critical difference is choice and free-will.

External algorithms assume the ego is in control, analyzing our behaviors to predict outcomes based on who we have been. But the ego resists change, clinging to what is familiar. In doing so, it limits our potential for true evolution. To break free from these limitations, we must reclaim the power of choice and embrace our own individual capacity for growth.

As conscious beings of light, we act as conduits for Source and its Divine Order, embracing a universal mission to restore harmony whenever disorder disrupts our world. We are instruments of balance in a landscape that is perpetually shifting, responding to the rhythms of existence.

The experiences we attract into our lives serve as mirrors, revealing the essence of our true selves and peeling away the layers of illusion we have constructed. These reflections highlight the battles we wage externally, illustrating how they echo the unresolved conflicts simmering within us.

We often attract the very resistance we judge, pulling in the opposite force and creating a cycle that persists until we learn to break free from its grip.

There are whispers of a great divide approaching—a time when many will rally to fight for the light against darkness, oblivious to the fact that we can easily become villains in our own narratives. This hero's bias entraps us in the matrix of the mind, leading us to believe we are champions of good, even as our interpretation of "good" often serves our own interests.

Much like an eye blind to its own reflection, we can remain oblivious to the truth about our nature. Yet, divine wisdom is ever-present in our relationships; we need only remain open to receive it when the moment is ripe.

Change is inevitable and should be embraced, not feared. Life isn't just about survival; it's about surrendering to the unknown, trusting the process, and viewing each transformation as an opportunity for deeper alchemy and connection.

In this Grand Design, nothing occurs by mere chance; every event plays a crucial role. By transcending judgment and embracing love and acceptance, we can enter a new dimension of existence. Instead of fighting against the tides, we must turn inward, nurturing our emotional and spiritual intelligence, and ultimately embodying the change we wish to see in the world.

This journey of integration invites us to confront our unexpressed emotions and articulate the words we have left unsaid. As the ego begins to crack open, a revolution of the self unfolds naturally. Through this sacred process, suffering is transmuted into purpose, fostering profound soul evolution into greater embodiment of spiritual maturity.

While judgment breeds suffering, it is through that very suffering that enlightenment emerges. As we learn to alchemize pain into wisdom, our hearts awaken to thought, and our minds begin to feel. In this harmonious state, the river of wisdom flows freely, allowing the universe, **the eternal philosopher**, to glean insights from our unique perspectives.

Each one of us contributes to the collective knowledge of the cosmos through our experience of the human condition, leaving an indelible mark on the Akashic Records and the very fabric of time.

When viewed from a higher perspective, chaos transforms into a powerful catalyst for growth. By elevating our individual consciousness, we gain insight into the interconnectedness of all things. Every experience—be it messy or serene—adds to the greater whole, the One.

This awareness fosters a sense of unity, revealing that every challenge, joy, and lesson is part of the same unfolding reality.

If we choose to accept the elements of duality instead of resisting them, we dissolve the illusion of separation and step into the fullness of our true essence. In this awakening, we reclaim our identity and purpose in human evolution, recognizing ourselves as a merging force of consciousness—the I AM (Awareness Manifested) within the Infinite Intelligence of the All.

Every day, I find myself in awe of the beauty our planet offers, the kindness that blossoms through generosity, and the wonder ignited by imagination. This realm, where magic thrives, beckons us to celebrate, cherish, and immerse ourselves fully in every fleeting moment.

In a world rife with turmoil yet rich in potential, we face a profound choice: to cultivate heaven on Earth or succumb to the confines of our own personal imprisonment.

Each moment is a chance to decide—will we choose love, hope, and connection, or will we fall into fear, isolation, and despair? The power to shape our reality resides within us, guiding our energy toward a vibrant, harmonious existence or entangling us in cycles of trauma and limitation.

We are the architects of our experiences; our beliefs sculpt the world around us with every thought, emotion, action, and intention. The paths we choose not only dictate our personal experiences but also send ripples throughout the world around us.

In this intricate web of life, we are called to awaken, harnessing our innate strength to transform chaos into beauty and despair into possibility.

The evolution of human consciousness begins with a reconnection to the innocence of our inner child, the essence of who we were before life molded us. In this pure space, we cultivate the courage to live with self-awareness, love, and integrity. Through this journey, we become the reflection of the world we aspire to create, embodying the very change we wish to see.

Why? *Because every child matters and deserves to thrive, receiving the emotional and spiritual intelligence we emit to help them flourish.* Each star child carries the codes for human evolution, and it is our sacred duty to nurture their radiance, guiding them to progress into the highest versions of self-mastery.

We must never let our divine light fade, as losing our enthusiasm for life suppresses our essence and hinders our evolution. Instead, we should embrace every moment, seeking inspiration and beauty, even in the smallest details.

Passion, excitement, and curiosity are the sparks that connect us to the language of physical reality and the guidance of our higher self. By acting on these impulses without attachment to specific outcomes, we maintain a state of optimism and flow, allowing growth and reflection to occur naturally.

Honest self-reflection and limiting belief systems are key to breaking negative patterns of the false feedback loop and aligning with our true purpose, rather than superficial desires.

The universe reflects our inner world, and through creativity and imagination, we can fully engage with life's opportunities, uniting mind, heart, and spirit in coherence.

Know thyself—you are the artist and the masterpiece of your creation, constantly evolving, a beautiful convergence of masculine and feminine, light and dark, day and night.

In the relationship of duality, we anchor unity consciousness—each aspect existing in harmony. It is through this delicate balance that we transcend the illusion of separation and bridge the gap to eternity.

This profound truth fuels my gratitude and drives my purpose, reminding me daily to cherish the gift of life.

Each of us holds the *Keys to Eternity*, enabling us to transform our shared reality by activating our *Coherent Heart.*

PART 2

Poetry For Embodiment

Understanding the Pain-Body

Truths in shadows lie,
Pain transformed, struggles depart,
Heart empowered, fly.

Alpha waves cascade,
Soothing pain's relentless grip–
Catalyst of growth.

Alpha Waves and Pain

When I'm in my pain-stricken frame,
I yearn for solace and relief from strife.
With alpha waves, I kindle healing's flame,
Guided by whispers of an inner life.

In solitude, I summon forth the key,
55515, a beacon in my mind's eye.
To soothe the ache that grips relentlessly,
And bring to bear powerful healings nigh.

The currents stir, a symphony unseen,
Within my being, they weave gentle sway.
Transforming anguish into tranquil sheen,
As pathways to renewal find their way.

Each moment lived ignites my soul's ascent,
Through spinal fields where energies arise.
From roots I filter, seeking light's intent,
And raise my stance beneath the cosmic skies.

In every trial, growth finds fertile ground,
As life's experiences shape and mold.
Our essence, through survival is bound,
And personal identity takes hold.

Yet in this process, reactivity's born,
Our hearts may turn defensive, harsh, cold.
Flight or fight may leave us feeling torn,
As growth beneath the cosmic skies unfolds.

So let us strive to balance and to see,
With steadfast will and harmony's embrace.
Beyond the reactive, find our true decree,
To seek wisdom that pain would dare efface.

In Eastern lore's realm,
Heart's rhythm, energies sway.
Qi dictates life's dance.

ARRHYTHMIA AND IMBALANCE

Within Eastern healing's ancient lore,
My heart's rhythm sings of energy in sway.
Where Qi and blood, the body's sacred store,
Dictate the dance of night and light of day.

The heart, esteemed as ruler in this plane,
Commands the flow of life through every part.
Yet when its balance falters, fraught with strain,
Arrhythmic beats ensue, disrupting art.

With Qi's decline, the heart may lose its way,
Palpitations stir, and anxiety takes hold.
Irregular beats in restless nights display,
As the vital force in shadows now grows cold.

Emotional stress can taint my heart's pure flow,
Its Qi disturbed by burdens deep and wide.
Prolonged strain seeds imbalances that grow,
And erratic beats in shadows may reside.

The heart field, when fraught with strain,
Becomes unsteady, drifting from its course.
Imbalances emerge, the rhythms wane,
As stress impedes my heart's harmonious force.

Thus, arrhythmia speaks to me of deeper signs,
In narratives of Qi, where wellness twines.

Bound energy knots,
Soul's entangled, trapped within.
Autoimmune cries.

Auto Immune Dis-ease

When there's a ruthless storm of conflict's wail,
Our nerves stand vigilant, a constant tale.
Awaiting each explosion, each strife-filled blast,
We live on edge, the calm never lasts.

Our bodies, weary, find no time to rest,
Autoimmune whispers, a silent pest.
Feeling attacked, oppressed, we fight,
Love's twisted darkness, blinding light.

In tangled webs of hurt, trust fades away,
Boundaries blurred, in disarray we sway.
No room to grow, expression's stifled plea,
Suppressing emotions, we live, not free.

Blockages form, in energy they bind,
A knotted mess within, our souls confined.
Survival's grip tight, in victim's guise,
Autoimmune battles, the body cries.

The dis-ease emerges, a relentless foe,
In the never-ending cycle, trapped, we know.
But in radical self-acceptance, we find the key,
To unlock the chains and set our spirits free.

In bitterness, emotions are unveiled,
Revealing depths of lessons to be learned.
Within its grip, profound truths are discerned,
As unresolved distress is finally unveiled.

Dis-ease, a teacher, guides on a path to find,
Inner peace where healing leaves us aligned.
Though the journey is long and may be unclear,
We honor strength and courage, the soul's frontier.

Muscles tense, spine pulled,

Tension knots, deeper woes thrive.

Confidence shattered.

Back Pain and Resentment

Eastern wisdom reveals how aches unveil,
When back pain's inner strife is concealed.
Disrupted Qi where harmony fails,
Taints the life force, its flow unsealed.

Muscles tighten, pulling spine astray,
In knots of tension, deeper woes are rife.
A shield against life's blows, in disarray,
Our confidence, stability, cut like a knife.

In the grip of resentment, we master the art,
Of transmuting victimhood to inner might.
Through trials endured, we kindle our own light,
Emerging stronger from life's turbulent chart.

Yet in this pain lies wisdom to be found,
A message whispered in the body's plea.
When thoughts soften, and energies unbound,
The grip of tension eases, sets us free.

Thus, in the dance of pain and harmony's art,
We find healing in the softening heart.

Tunnels bridging in,
Lungs constrict with doubt, inflamed.
Congested route, coughs.

Bronchitis and Lungs

When we suffer a loss and deny its roar,
Grief lingers, injuring the lung's tender core.
Yet hurt extends beyond bereavement's door,
A channel of bronchitis, it may implore.

The lungs, like tunnels, bridge inside and out,
Inflamed and constricted by internal doubt.
Obstacles build up, creating a congested route,
As mucus traps debris, sparking a coughing bout.

This defense serves well in its own plight,
Yet both inward and outward traffic takes flight.
Bronchitis hints at struggles we might fight,
Against emotions, tears, and the encroaching night.

Linked to the heart, this message rings clear,
We shun the pain, the loss, the tears.
It's an invitation to reflect, to steer,
Towards embracing emotions, without fear.

Body's tale, bruises,
Easily wrought, like petals.
Whispers of limits.

Bruising and Discomfort

In my body's tale, bruises paint the scene,
Easily wrought, like petals in the breeze.
Each mark a whisper of a boundary keen,
A vulnerability masked with ease.

Emotions swell, yet I suppress their rise,
A childhood echo, a people-pleasing mask.
Hurtful words, unseen tears in disguise,
A pattern etched, a challenging task.

Linked to the Earth, the spleen holds sway,
Its balance disrupted by wounds concealed.
To heal, to reprogram, day by day,
I reclaim my power, emotions revealed.

In discomfort, new paths come to light,
A chance to pivot to a fresh terrain.
Through anxiety's lens, I break the chain,
Finding strength to shift from plight to flight.

Through inner work, I find my voice anew,
Expressing truth, in grace, and breakthrough.

Inside, virus lurks,
Fiery sprite, the truth demands.
Shadows revealed.

Cold Sores and Anger

In moments when our boundaries are strained,
Cold sores emerge, like whispers of unrest.
Around the mouth, points of pain maintained,
Creating distance, where emotions wrest.

A time for self-reflection, to explore,
Anger simmers if our limits are crossed.
These sores, eruptions unexpressed, implore,
A voice unheard, a message deep embossed.

Perhaps a pattern from our youthful years,
Or resonance of exhaustion, wounds untold.
Saying no, establishing firm frontiers,
Are acts of self-care, not heart grown cold.

Within, a virus lurks, a fiery sprite,
Demanding truth, from shadows long concealed.
The inner-child's fury, burning, hot and bright,
Exposing secrets, yet to be revealed.

In anger's heat, acceptance finds its birth,
A tempest churns, revealing paths anew.
Through fiery trials, we learn to construe,
The situation's fact, its weight and worth.

So, heed the message of this burning sore,
To speak our truth and close the unhealed door.

Frustration rises,
Dominant, strong, tension deep.
Imbalance in life.

Cramps and Stagnation

Cramps in the light body ring like alarm bells,
A stark reminder of rigidity's sway.
Where stagnation lurks, and freedom quells,
Joy's absence felt in the light of day.

Frustration rises, dominant and strong,
A call to ponder what stirs this tension deep.
Work's weight, imbalance, a life without song,
Leaving little room for joy to seep.

Yet in this turmoil lies a chance to see,
The power within to shift and rearrange.
To break through binds, to let the spirit free,
And in the dance of change, find joy's range.

Emotions swell, a tempest in the soul,
As muscles tense with each relentless ache.
Yearning for release, to feel once whole,
Yet trapped within, a silent plea to make.

Qi's flow disrupted, fields blocked with pain,
Blood stasis grips, a shadow in the night.
In pathways constricted, where energies wane,
Cramps speak of battles fought in silent fight.

Yet in this turmoil lies a trail to find,
To heal the wounds that linger in the mind.

Loss strikes, the heart feels cold,
Depression's cloak hides the pain–
Shadows dim the soul.

Emotional Loss and Flow

When loss hath struck, and freeze is the frame,
Depression's cloak shields the wounded heart,
For severed ties, the soul doth bear the blame,
In shadows deep, where light cannot impart.

Connection, a vital thread that binds us tight,
It shapes our days, our nights, our very core.
Devoid of which, we stumble in the night,
In grief's embrace, we find ourselves at war.

Belonging, bonding, essence of our being,
They guide our steps, our hunger, and rest.
Without their warmth, we find ourselves unseeing,
Lost spirits adrift, by sorrow's winds caressed.

Yet pain and grief, they are friends indeed,
To mend broken hearts, they're allies in our need.

Unhealthy pursuits,
Ensnare souls with cunning chains.
Comfort turns to pain.

Fleeting Pleasures

What is addiction, and how does it thrive?
When boundaries break, we seek a swift escape.
In fleeting comforts, we strive to stay alive,
A refuge found, a solace for pain's scrape.

From food to substances, desires take hold,
An illusion of relief, yet truth untold.
We chase fleeting pleasures, but find despair,
Trapped in a cycle that seems beyond repair.

Disconnected from the heart's true light,
We wander lost in shadows deep and cold.
Old scars resurface in the dead of night,
As wounds unhealed leave distress to unfold.

But in the crucible of struggle, hope remains,
With courage and love, we break the chains.
Healing begins, with each brave step we take,
Restoring life's essence, our spirit awakes.

Addiction marks where Qi no longer flows,
A blockage in the body's sacred streams.
Where once pure energy now falters, slows,
And health gives way to fractured dreams.

Addiction signals Qi that's gone astray,
While self-love guides us to harmony's way.

Guard, bold decisions,
Guides judgments with steady hand.
Courage, strength unfold.

Gallbladder & Decision Making

Within our being, the gallbladder reigns,
A force profound, beyond its bile's employ.
Its essence spans through time's unbounded plains,
Guiding decisions with an unwavering ploy.

A keeper of decisions, clear and bold,
It guides our judgments with a steady hand.
In its domain, courage and strength unfold,
As visions of the future firm, we stand.

With eyes that see beyond here and now,
It governs clarity, a mental light.
But imbalances may furrow thought's brow,
And cloud the mind, obscuring insight bright.

Expressive grace, its balance true,
Resilience blooms in its hallowed space.
Yet fear, a specter, dims the inner view,
Leaving us trapped in life's relentless race.

In calm authenticity, we find release,
Guided by life's gentle, flowing stream.
Decision's burden eased, our souls at peace,
As gallbladder's woes dissolve in the dream.

For when fear's grip relinquishes its hold,
Life's guidance shines, a beacon brightly bold.

Throbbing, pounding head,
Qi's waltz meets turmoil's strife.
Pressure's tempest, pain.

HEADACHES AND PRESSURE

Inside my throbbing, pounding head,
Qi's delicate waltz meets turmoil's strife.
Pressure's tempest, dietary thread,
Disrupting the flow brings agony to life.

Emotional storms, to my eyesight's dismay,
Disturbs the harmony, the balance frails.
External forces in their fierce array,
Smog, clouds, rain, their havoc assail.

Along meridians, where energies wane,
I feel the pulse of imbalance, sirens bold.
Various triggers cause nausea with disdain,
Emotional stress takes its fiery hold.

Within this realm, pain's sensations reign,
Imbalances disrupt the brain's domain.
Blood vessels constrict, then swell again,
A symphony of chaos, endless chain.

Serotonin, the conductor of pain,
Guiding the vessels with its subtle hand.
In this delicate dance, a loss, a gain,
Migraine's cruel grip, a ruthless command.

Yet relief remains within the herbal art,
A remedy for nature's soothing hand.
To calm the liver's storm, to cool the heart,
And guide the flow where harmony is planned.

In eastern wisdom's ancient, sacred lore,
Hope blooms anew to ease my suffering's core.

Heartburn tale unfolds,
Acid upward takes its flight.
Inflammation blooms.

Heartburn and Indigestion

Indigestion brings a message that's bold,
Where the stomach's fire erupts and reigns.
This vital force breaks down food's hold,
Assisting absorption with its flaming gain.

Yet when heartburn strikes, a tale untold,
Acid, misguided, takes an upward flight.
Inflammation blooms, a bitter scold,
As it moves against the natural light.

In this upheaval, our hearts should probe,
Our inner realms, where worries roam.
Reflection is key, where emotions strobe,
For therein lies the root of digestive foam.

Within, we must search, our souls explore,
What churns beneath, where worries graze.
The echo calls sensations to the fore,
Root of digestive strife in tangled maze.

To heal, we must confront the flames we tend,
Restore the peace, let troubled waters mend.

Hives alarm, breach shown,
Siren's wail, imbalance warned.
Urgent signal preached.

Hives and Imbalance

Upon our skin, our body's sacred shield,
Hives sound alarms when borders are breached.
Like sirens wail, their warning cries revealed,
A signal of imbalance urgently preached.

Urticaria, they're called in ancient tongue,
A tale of Qi disturbed its flow awry.
Red welts arise, in patterns wild and sprung,
A rave of discomfort, drawing sigh.

Within, the body's fortress under siege,
Mistaken warriors ravage without cease.
Healthy cells, leaked by the immune's intrigue,
In this battleground, they find no peace.

To soothe the storm, we must attend with care,
Avoiding allergic triggers that stoke the flame.
Spicy, greasy temptations, beware,
Instead, detoxing foods we acclaim.

In balance lies the key to skin's reprieve,
With stress at bay, our wellness we achieve.

Mindful practice brings
Release from stress, tranquil mind.
Hormonal peace found.

Hormonal Disparity

When midlife crisis knocked on my door,
Hormonal imbalance began life's race.
Yin and Yang disrupted my fragile form,
In Qi and blood disharmony took place.

Liver and kidney bear the weight of woe,
Their rhythms strained by life's relentless call.
Irregular cycles, emotions flow,
Fatigue and migraines, shadows of the fall.

In every motion, a whispered drawl,
To harmonize the rhythms deep within.
With breath as guide, we heed the inner thrall,
And let the Qi's gentle flow begin.

For disappointment bears treasures to find,
A path to liberation, to let things go.
Through shattered hopes, new wisdom grows,
Guiding us to leave the past behind.

Through mindful practice, stress finds its release,
As tranquil waters soothe the troubled mind.
In this serene realm, hormonal peace,
And balanced energies, in union bind.

Thus, in the sanctuary of this embrace,
Mind-body practice is a healing grace.

Imbalance burdens,
Craving connection, shunning.
Loneliness grips tight.

Circulation and Loneliness

In each heartbeat, my journey commences,
Through veins and arteries, life's vital stream.
Blood, the essence of life, in its defense,
Nourishes each cell like a gentle dream.

In lore of old, it's the body's sacred space,
A vital substance, cherished in its flow.
Nurturing organs, with gentle grace,
Balancing the Qi of life, aglow.

Yet when imbalance strikes, its weight I bear,
Craving connection, shunning solitude.
Emotionally adrift, burdened with care,
In loneliness grip, my spirit subdued.

Sadness, its constant companion, I find,
Whispers of despair, in silence it's heard.
"Set me free," it cries in heart and mind,
From isolation's grip where light is obscured.

Yet amidst this turmoil, a flicker of hope,
An opportunity to reclaim the trope.
This is a moment for our soul's resurrection,
Where truth and essence find connection.

Cells roam, multiply,
Hope turned stone, invasion's home.
Ageless murmurs groan.

Lump of Toxicity

Amidst life's tangled web, there lies,
A foe that strikes with stealth and grim disguise.
Cancer, it's called, a scourge we can't ignore,
Spreading its grip, leaving hearts sore.

Abnormal cells, they multiply and roam,
Invading tissues, turning hope to stone.
No age is spared, its reach is unbound,
From youth to elder, the murmurs resound.

But oft it lurks in those who selflessly give,
Nurturers, caretakers, in whom it may live.
Within their breasts, a hidden lump may lie,
A silent plea beneath a caring eye.

Inside us all, a child's voice does yearn,
For love, for nurture, for freedom to learn.
Yet when ignored, that innocence cries,
Trapped and suffocated, 'neath the skies.

Unmet needs, the softest parts are scarred,
In silence and stress, our souls are marred.
But when toxicity surfaces, it's a call,
To change, to reflect, to break down the wall.

In shadows cast by trembling doubts, we find
The whispered lessons fear would have us learn.
Within its grasp, a spark of growth does burn,
A call to rise where timid hearts are confined.

So, heed the message, unleash, and shine,
Express, release, let emotions entwine.
For in facing our fears, we find our strength,
To rise above the toxicity, no matter the length.

Painful cycles hold,
Mind and body conflict bold.
Life's flow drained, tug war.

Menstrual Cycle

Within the rhythm of womanhood's embrace,
Menstrual flow, a vital, sacred grace.
Reflecting Qi and Yin, Yang's dance,
In the interplay, life's cosmic expanse.

Flowering organs unite in harmony,
Liver, spleen, kidneys, in symphony.
Linked to our light bodies, a sacred tie,
A reminder of our power, reaching high.

Hormones, the messengers, respond in kind,
To thoughts, emotions, perceptions entwined.
Energetic charges in the blood, they sail,
Releasing past burdens, emotions frail.

Yet anger, stress, frustration tightly wound,
Hold onto blood, making release confound.
Resentment, chronic, lingering, severe,
Weighs on our health, a shadow we fear.

Painful cycles, when injustice we hold,
Conflict between mind and body, bold.
The tug of war, draining life's sweet flow,
An intense burden, in pain's cruel throes.

And heavy flow, a sign of deeper plight,
Exhaustion, joylessness, stressful bite.
So let us listen, to our body's plea,
Find balance in mind, soul, and body, all three.

Neck, bridge seen and sought,
Vision to future it brought.
Spasms, wake-up call.

Neck Stiffness and Guilt

In the aftermath of shock and stress, I find,
A sudden pang, my neck in pain entwined.
As my eyes cast down, my body starts to sway,
Adapting swiftly to where my gaze may lay.

The neck, a bridge between the seen and sought,
Allows my vision to the future port.
But sometimes, spasms seize with sharp distress,
A wake-up call, to life's changes, no less.

When the light body speaks, I see,
Resistance to the shifts, uneasy I be.
Emotionally, reacting to the storm,
Of unexpected news, life's twisting form.

In guilt's fierce storm, a compass for my soul,
Reveals when my values stray awry.
Through the tempest's howl, I heed the inner cry,
Nudging back to where I'm meant to stroll.

These whispers from within my being rise,
Emotions surge, unveiling life's disguise.
Unexpected news, trials, and tests,
Compel me to confront the unknown nests.

Suddenly, we're forced to turn our sight,
Towards a place unknown, beyond our might.
A time for self-reflection, in the mist,
Letting go of control, with self-love kissed.

For though we can't foresee what lies ahead,
Great positive shifts may rise from what we dread.

Harsh bonds come to light,
Connection to self mends life–
Darkness yields to dawn.

Pain Body and Connection

In the quest for knowledge, the mind we prize,
Above the body, where emotion lies.
We've honed the power to override,
The whispers of the heart, by logic's stride.

Disconnected from our spirits deep,
In tangled webs of experience, we keep.
Normalized, this disjunction seems to be,
Between our essence and our reality.

We've grown comfortable with pains hum,
Expecting suffering, as years drum.
Suppressing urges, numbing what we feel,
It has become the norm, our fate to seal.

But our pain body, in their silent plea,
Shout through discomfort, to set us free.
For pain reveals the battle within,
Ego versus truth, a war to win.

Survival mode obscures our inner light,
Hidden beneath the mask we wear so tight.
Unseen, unheard, yet longing to be found,
Our authentic selves, on sacred ground.

Suffering shows a bond that's harsh and strained,
Yet connection with life brings healing unrestrained.

Negative thoughts breed,
Chaos in the heart's domain.
Imbalance takes lead.

Physical Imbalances

Negative thoughts, imbalance it breeds,
Creating chaos, where the heart once heeds.
Belief in self-care, deemed selfish, untrue,
Leads to neglect, from our essence askew.

Boundaries fade, as disconnection reigns,
From body's whispers, lost in the strains.
Nurturing all, but our own souls' plea,
Leaves us adrift, from true harmony, free.

Exhaustion grips, while digestion falters,
In tangled thoughts, our essence alters.
Our light bodies, reflecting every thought,
Reveal the battles that we have fought.

Yet meeting needs, not selfish, but essential,
A belief ingrained, deemed preferential.
Passed down through generations, old and wise,
Yet truth resides within our own heart's guise.

When self-compassion blooms, healing starts,
Guiding others with love, from the heart.

Skin, boundary's art,
Reflects turmoil in heart's chart.
Emotions lie thin.

Psoriasis and Powerlessness

When we feel trapped, our bodies cry,
An inflamed response, where sorrows lie.
Skin cells in haste, their cycle whirls around,
Urgency within, red patches abound.

This irritation speaks of anger's flame,
And frustrations held, where we assign blame.
The back of the head, burdened with the past,
And thoughts that linger, shadows they cast.

Skin, boundary between our worlds apart,
Reflects the turmoil, etched upon the heart.
Suppressed emotions, hidden deep within,
Emerge as patches, where struggles begin.

Psoriasis' message, clear and plain,
Reflect on disturbances, break the chain.
The inner child echoes, voice so frail,
Longing to break free from doubt's dark veil.

Energetic flow,

Keeps wellness high and low.

Blockages disrupt stream.

Qi or Vital Life Force Energy

In the tapestry of life, Qi threads its way,
The essence of existence, night, and day.
It pulses through all, both near and far,
The essence of life, the guiding star.

Invisible channels, meridians they're named,
Where Qi flows, unending and untamed.
Connecting organs, tissues, with ease,
Ensuring health, the body's harmonies.

Smooth and balanced, this energetic flow,
Keeps wellness intact, both high and low.
But blockages arise, disrupt the stream,
Bringing disharmony, a painful dream.

To understand health, illness, and cure,
Qi's the key, of this we can be sure.
In traditional wisdom, its power is seen,
In every living being, in every scene.

Battles rage within,
Desire meets shame, voices din.
Tears, inflammation.

Ribs and Unworthiness

My childhood wounds cut deep and raw,
I clutch pain like a blanket, my only straw.
As chances to grow emerge in the light,
Fear floods in, panic grips, an endless fight.

Identifying with hurt, I shrink and cower,
Avoiding growth, trapped in its power.
Panic strikes, chest spasms, a painful call,
As I seek to expand, to break down the wall.

Internal battles rage, desire meets doubt,
Voices of criticism, I can't live without.
Tears and inflammation, where ribs protect,
Guardians of my heart, in pain, I reflect.

Excruciating agony, vulnerability's glare,
Exposed, defenseless, my wounds laid bare.
Shame's grasp tightens, binding with might,
Self-worth cloaked in darkness, lost in the night.

In self-reflection's mirror, clarity appears,
To broaden horizons, expand and grow.
Opening my heart to authenticity's glow,
Releasing unworthiness, freedom nears.

Impossible choice,
Rooted patterns undeniable.
Voiceless, confined, trapped.

Sinus and Postnasal Drip

In phlegm's defense, against pathogens it stands,
Shielding our inner world with steadfast hands.
Yet in our sinus cavity it blocks,
When life's demand overwhelm in flocks.

Postnasal drip, a sign of inner strife,
When pressures mount, disrupting inner life.
Invasion of privacy, burdens weigh,
Exposure, offense, in disarray.

Faced with choices that seem impossible,
Rooted in patterns, feelings undeniable.
Unable to voice dislikes, we're confined,
Trapped in circumstances, body, and mind.

A time for self-reflection, to delve deep,
In emotional currents, our secrets keep.
Release the blockages, let light's flow start,
And heal the wounds that linger in the heart.

In depths of silence,
Is sacred sanctuary,
Urging us to shift.

The Uterus and Regret

Within the womb's soft cradle, creation stirs,
A space of stillness where new life occurs.
From Yin's gentle embrace, Yang's light ignites,
In the quiet of dreams, where hope takes flight.

The uterus, a haven for growth and grace,
Where life blossoms in its sacred space.
From the depths of silence, dreams arise,
In this sacred sanctuary, where love lies.

When pain intrudes, a whisper to explore,
The pelvis, where emotions often pour.
Breathing deeply, feeling tensions ease,
In the womb's embrace, find inner peace.

The regrets may echo, urging a shift,
A chance to alter course, accept anew.
Through its weight, pathways break through,
Guiding toward horizons yet to lift.

Noticing tensions, emotions confined,
Yearning for release, within the mind.
Connecting with this essence, we find peace,
Regulating cycles, our worries cease.

Light body unveils,
Hole where sadness, fear reside.
Anxiety's flight.

Vertigo and Sadness

Vertigo, a dance of inner disharmony,
A tale of Qi and unbalanced symphony.
In the delicate scale of Yin and Yang's sway,
Vertigo may find its unwelcome stay.

Rooted in patterns of internal strife,
The spleen's weakness, a player in life.
Transforming food to Qi and blood's embrace,
Deficiency here may lead to vertigo's chase.

The light body reveals a hole unseen,
Where sadness bears the lack we crave.
Anxiety's wings take flight, worry's wave,
Ungrounded we falter, stability's sheen.

In the kidney's root, weakness may lie,
A gap in the energetic field, we cannot deny.
To tame vertigo's wild, chaotic spin,
Reduce stress, rest, for balanced life to begin.

When we quiet our mind, with wellness as our guide,
We restore harmony, where vertigo may reside.

Opposites entwine,
Forces interconnect, bind.
Harmony's balance.

Yin and Yang

Within life's intricate, woven design,
Yin and Yang entangle, a waltz profound.
They shape our vision, concepts so divine,
In the duality that's always been around.

In constant motion, these forces reside,
Bound by a cosmic, enchanting spell.
Their sway brings coherence, order beside,
From deep chaos, they weave their tale.

In ancient days, eastern breezes blow,
With fables of healing from times of yore.
Yin and Yang, in unity they show,
Guiding life's rhythm to its very core.

Oh, ageless wisdom, in healing's art,
Deep mysteries and stories are yet untold.
In whispers heard when shadows depart,
Yin and Yang's embrace, our essence bold.

To heal, we strive to mend flow's soft hum,
Restoring balance, easing each ache's strain.
For in the dance of Yin and Yang's sum,
Lies the key to wellness, in harmony's domain.

Realizing Vital Relationships

Unlock happiness,
Be your own truest ally,
Friendship within, thrive.

Heart's tale gently told,
Golden age in warmth and grace.
Melody and love.

A Golden Age

Within my heart's chambers, a tale unfolds,
The golden age echoes in senses bold.
Smooth and hot, like a polished metal's grace,
Sunlight's beam engulfs in a warm embrace.

A melody arises, a delicate bell's chime,
Or a finely balanced instrument, a tune sublime.
Luxury surrounds me in life's joyful ballet,
Loved ones envelop, in safety we stay.

Tastes like soothing honey, a decadent treat,
Champagne kisses bubbles in this glitter's fleet.
It's a sensory journey, in delight's sweet trance,
In imagination, these moments gently enhance.

In the plasma light's harmonious waves,
The golden age retells, peace it engraves.
Soft and fiery, like polished metal's grace,
In my heart's chamber, this tale I embrace.

Alchemy within,

Mind surrenders; heart breaks through.

Self-love frolics free.

Higher Purpose

Upon the stage of self, I take my part,
To unveil purpose, a journey to start.
From depths within, brilliance unconfined,
A radiant soul, in joy enshrined.

Unlocking treasures, a rarest find,
Thriving in abundance, heart, and mind.
In joy's sweet embrace, my spirit soars,
A luminous soul, life's grand amour.

No reasons bind, just genius pure,
Alive, for being, a truth to assure.
In higher purpose, I find my song,
A dance of existence, where I belong.

Reveling in the grandeur of this quest,
My purpose displays life's bequest.
This journey expands with a mystic grace,
Embarking into the heart's enchanted space.

Authority of thought, a paradigm's hold,
Yields to the heart, where mysteries unfold.
Unlocking higher purpose, a sacred art,
A transformation, mystical from the start.

In self's alchemy, fusion true,
Mind surrenders, heart breaks through.
A waltz of essence, a spiritual trance,
This process yields cosmic dance.

Turning inward, where the mystic lies,
Within the soul's sanctuary, the spirit flies.
The most vital relationship of all,
Is the love of self, this realm's sacred call.

A journey unfolds, a profound odyssey,
Deserving love, a revelation to decree.

Shadows whisper gifts,
Light codes weave a tale untold.
Alchemy unfolds.

Shadow's Gift

In shadows cast, a hidden gift lies deep,
Heart's whisper in light codes softly creep.
A twist, mysterious, in our human tale,
Myths and fables weave, a story's sail.

The seed of suffering, within our being sown,
Basis for tales in every myth we've known.
Embrace the shadows, let their essence speak,
Gifts within, the alchemy we seek.

Acceptance blooms, shadows then reveal,
Healing murmurs that time cannot conceal.
True nature awakened, a creative stream,
In DNA's rave, a new impulse gleam.

A subtle mutation, cells rearrange,
Biochemistry shifts, a potent change.
Transforming shadows, a leap profound,
Perspective shifts in a quantum bound.

Transformation's tale,
Mask cast aside, unburdened,
The epoch of change.

Life's Arcade

Amidst self-discovery's gentle grace,
I found a haven, a serene space.
No shadows to tighten their embrace,
Openness bloomed, a rhythmic chase.

Life's relentless abyss, a tale foregone,
Joy's enchantment, a melody dawned.
Above the mist, I soared, reborn,
Cherishing love, memories worn.

At the crossroads of choice so clear,
Courage ousted ego's lurking fear.
Kindness guided, drawing me near,
Through life's arcade, I persevere.

In the epoch of change, I stood unveiled,
Work stressors faded, my spirit exhaled.
Embracing self-worth, no longer assailed,
Freedom reigns, vulnerability hailed.

Layer by layer, old façades I shed,
In the naked truth, my soul widespread.
I became the light, no longer misled,
With Divine's caress, my spirit fed.

With newfound purpose, I am unbound,
Unshackled from what once weighed me down.
A sacred bond with myself I've crowned,
Boundless and limitless, in harmony found.

Formless force I am,
Fluid vessel in life's wave,
Embracing each change.

Fluid Vessel

In the realm reversed, I carve my sanctuary,
Learning from primary bonds, a foundation.
With courage, I unravel threads of time,
Shifting paradigms, containing energies sublime

I am akin to water, crafting my own vessel,
Fluidity embodied in the dance of change.
Within my biome, complexities intertwine,
A continuous flow, orchestrated existence.

Water shapes behavior, unseen conductor,
Human actions echo in their rhythmic cycle.
The sun's energy and gravity's pull,
Propel me forward in harmony with Earth.

Without resistance, water moves in grace,
No solid walls obstruct their chosen path.
It journeys freely, an unstoppable force,
An essence constant, patient in its course.

It wears away the unyielding stone,
A testament to endurance, a quiet triumph.
Alone and free, in the fluidity of existence,
A reflection of patience silently persisted.

I AM water, harnessing shapeless power,
A fluid vessel within life's intricate wave.
This story's etched in my virtual ecosystem,
A container holding each adaptable change.

My worth is laid bare,
In vulnerability's face.
Paradigm shifts, grace.

TRUE ESSENCE

The expanse of life, my vital tie,
I ponder the vessel, the soul's melody.
A cornerstone for bonds, both far and nigh,
A nucleus composing, balanced free.

The plea of my inner child, in softness heard,
Frames unearthed from a distant yore.
A profound bond within, my being stirred,
A true compass, guiding me evermore.

Two paths unveiled beneath the glowing light,
Ego's shadow or healing's upward flight.
With courage, I chose the route so bright,
Integration's road, wisdom's guiding light.

When contrast slices into my heart's space,
My worth laid bare in vulnerability's face.
Steered by love Divine, old bonds erase,
Paradigms shift, a newfound refined grace.

Upon life's journey, threads of my design,
Growth and awareness weave a tapestry fine.
True essence diffuses with a warm rasp,
Hope takes root in sacred light's firm grasp.

I illuminate my path to glorious flowering,
Union with my own Divinity, empowering.
My eyes blaze with the fire of pure knowing,
Deep compassion, fearless freedom showing.

Rising triumphant from cocoons of the past,
Metamorphosis complete, the change is vast.
In self's brilliance, I stand steadfast,
Entering a journey destined to last.

Openness unfolds,
Where Eden's paradise grows.
Sailing to light shores.

Eden's Bridge

Inside the center field, a bridge unfurls,
'Twixt earthly bounds, cosmic, swirling pearls.
Eden's secret garden, in auras sown,
A dance of energy, a realm unknown.

Burden in lung's meridian, bears the load,
Of grief repressed, a weight in life's abode.
Yet, in freedom found, it sheds density's ties,
Assuming lightness, 'neath expansive skies.

Symbolic is the bridge, a sacred link,
Uniting spirit and matter in a rhythmic sync.
Breath's anchor calls, a hero's journey starts,
Guiding imbalanced vibes from the central heart.

Through toroidal fields, in profound release,
A sacred sonnet appears crowned with light.
Letting go, freed, releasing ties that strain,
Untangling bonds, shedding emotional load.

Nurturing connections, a fresh genesis,
A path bestowed with ease and openness.
Relationships that breathe, mutually shared,
A waltz of souls where energies just flow.

No longer burdened by the chaotic sea,
I sail towards shores of open tranquility,
Where bonds are light, yet strong in unity.

Let healthy ties evolve, a symphony,
A harmonious connection, a sweet decree,
Where hearts align in perfect reciprocity.

Genetic strands bond,
Yin and Yang foundation strong.
Holographic codes.

Wells of Introspect

There is a labyrinth of the inner self,
Where mirrors held reveal our true wealth.
Our sense of being, the essence, the stealth,
Defines our purpose, shapes our very health.

In this looking glass of self-concept wide,
Perception weaves a fabric, thought guide.
How we esteem, success or failure's tide,
Determines the path where we'll coincide.

Delve deep within, the wells of introspect,
Unveil the layers of intrinsic aspects.
Uncover views and feelings, reconnect,
The strength inside, our essence is perfect.

Our cells, custodians of ages past,
Hold memories, secrets destined to last.
Encoded within, a cosmic tapestry,
Harmonious stars in unity, set free.

Genetic code, two strands entwined,
Foundation of Yin and Yang combined.
A holographic microcosm defined,
Memories in cells, destinies enshrined.

Imagination, the key to freedom's door,
Facing fears, ancestral ties I tore.
Cells are listening, antennae galore,
Responding to shifts, the genetic core.

Embrace thyself, value light's warm glow,
A sense of oneness, a life to sow.
Through the cosmic tapestry, let it flow,
A rebirth of balance, radiant life to show.

My acceptance's grace,
Cornerstone of self's strength shines.
Imperfections bind.

ACCEPTANCE

By accepting myself, real peace I find,
A fortress strong, a spirit unconfined.
Embracing flawlessness, stories unfold,
Within humanity's fabric, a tale retold.

No perfect mortal exists, this truth I hold,
Life's lessons escort on its winding road.
In blunders, wisdom may find its mold,
Enhancing my sense of self, stories retold.

At a quantum level, fate's not my decree,
My attitude shapes the reality I see.
Self-concept's beacon, clarity ablaze,
Unlocking potential in an unwavering gaze.

This mirror reflects my truest essence,
Critiques are ripples, in my presence.
Confidently I tread the path unknown,
Grounded in self-love, seeds are sown.

Against adversity's stare, I stand alone,
Humming my tune, a melody of my own.
So let surrender guide me through the night,
Traversing shadows, ready for flight.

With every step, my true self in sight,
Knowing within lies the power to alight.

Beyond ego's play,
Quest for essence, truths cascade,
Pure nature embraced.

Contemplation

In my beguiled odyssey by the stream's soft gleam,
Between musing's calm and attention's keen beam.
Internally I roam, in embrace reflective,
A waltz of spirit, through pathways elective.

I seize the moment for contemplation's tune,
Merging with meditation, resonating monsoon.
Entwined with life's tales, a gentle reply,
Discerning lessons in the wind's tender sigh.

To know myself, past the ego's masquerade,
A journey into essence, where truths cascade.
Accepting pure nature, harmonious kin,
Dancing in rhythm with the universal spin.

To contemplate, a word with roots divine,
A temple for thoughts, in spaces where I twine.
In fleeting times, where perceptions bloom,
I ponder life, in its serene mystical room.

This profound exploration is a sacred art,
Unveiling mysteries, a journey of my heart.
In whispers soft, where reflections dance,
I found my essence, life's true romance.

In darkness, a spark,

Love's touch, soothing wounded hearts.

Whispers of wholeness.

Love's Presence

Among tangled thoughts, my mind's embrace,
Love's gentle touch begins its subtle trace.
Soft whispers unravel life's intricate maze,
My spirit finds solace through the low tides' gaze.

In moments unseen, love's presence endures,
Lingering, extending its ethereal cures.
A lifeline unyielding, serene reassures,
Reminding me I'm part of a cosmic tour.

In darkness, flickers emerge, a delicate grace,
Divine touch, a balm for hearts' tender space.
Concealed, yet constant, it leaves no trace,
In wholeness where wounds are sewn into place.

With free will, I choose to expand,
Accepting devotion, weaving life's strand.
No change or event dim love's luminous brand,
A solace brightening my heart's worn land.

So let it radiate, this ballad of my core,
Absolute love, my guiding star's lore.
In its tender embrace, finding strength to soar,
A beacon of light, ever near, evermore.

Self-love's chapter blooms,
Nurturing time, untold worth.
Essence honored, seen.

Art of Devotion

Oh, self-devotion, a sacred path to tread,
A dedication to our inner flame.
A commitment to nourish heart and head,
To respect self, unsubscribing from shame.

In this chapter, love for self does bloom,
Nurturing our time and values are untold.
Essence honored, a presence to behold,
Wellness practiced, fulfillment's story told.

To prioritize self-care, not in vain,
But as a gift of Divine to our radiant soul.
With boundaries set, freedom we attain,
Falling in love with self, recalling the whole.

For with affection, our light doth shine,
The art of self-devotion's a blessed sign.
A path of reflection, perpetual and vast,
Deserving of joy, a promise that will last.

Admitting the good already in my life,
It's the basis for abundance, free from strife.
In the realm of gratitude, my heart takes flight,
A symphony of blessings, a dance of light.

Quest for truth unveils,
Authenticity's depth.
Wisdom gently flows.

Wisdom's Murmur

In the journey for truth, I ventured within,
Where the heart beats and emotions begin.
Battles fought fiercely in the soul's terrain,
To unearth myself, where shadows wane.

No hiding flaws, nor virtues in the shade,
In the raw essence of reality, feelings laid.
Through the ebb and flow of my cosmic loom,
Identity sculpted, projected from ego's groom.

Examining beliefs and convictions standing tall,
In vulnerability's embrace, the Angels call.
A steadfast self, weathering storms untold,
Guiding with courage, emotions controlled.

Down the river of time, wisdom gently flows,
In the heart's soft murmur, where emotion grows.
Acknowledging sorrow, not from life's throes,
But from the mind's illusion, the truth bestows.

Patterns weave our bonds,
Ending ties is self-respect.
Heartbreak, the lesson.

Getting Real

Relationships are patterns, bonds that sway,
Some linger too long, deaf to change's plea.
Attachments formed, a reenactment's play,
Reflecting the inner child's destiny.

External love may falter, remain incomplete,
Devoid of respect, truth, and openness sweet.
Prioritizing, valuing to make hearts replete,
In honor lies the nectar, love's essence to greet.

Connection, trust, safety, integrity's reign,
In relationships, these elements bind.
Sustaining vital bonds, they withstand strain,
A textile of endurance, intertwined.

Courage emerges to get real with truth,
To weigh if bonds uplift or chains constrain.
Choosing self, to retrace our lost youth,
In the unknown, a liberation to gain.

Unlearning the story of giving all,
Codependent deeds, fiercely loyal.
Emotional needs neglected, heart's silent toll.
Daring to end ties, pain of a wounded soul.

Refusing to settle for mere warmth at night,
Embracing the unknown with valor bright.
In the terror, liberation takes flight,
Earning connection that feels real and right.

With compassion, invested and true,
Walking away from what makes you blue.
Into the unknown, bravery anew,
Deserving a union that's worthy of you.

Codes, tales arise,
Chronicles from origin.
Self-revealed, mystic.

Beyond the Veil

Beyond the veil, we seek depths unknown,
In quest for truths that lie in realms unseen.
It is the substance of the souls we hone,
To reunite with Oneness, vast and keen.

Forgotten codes and tales begin to rise,
Origin chronicles, not just past life scenes.
Revealing self in cryptic, mystic guise,
Steering us on this journey, serene.

Within ourselves, a myriad of hues,
Both shadows and the light, in harmony.
Through flaws and virtues, we find clues,
To self-appreciation's brilliancy.

Uncover paths to greater cosmic source,
When shadows loom, let inner might emerge.
Embrace the unity, the divine force,
And liberate the spirit, a tidal surge.

The galaxies in motion, their intellect gleams,
Embedded in the core of our own cells.
Connected to the cosmic particles theme,
We are eternal, as the universe tells.

So let the flames rise, with passion ablaze,
In the warmth of self-love, our spirit sways.
For within, a fire, a force that's resilient,
Accepting our true self, the journey's brilliant.

Awareness is key,
Treasures found on Earth's vast realm.
Ballad of rebirth.

SELF-DISCOVERY

Forging a vital relationship, a self-dive starts,
Deep through valleys, where truths gently gleam.
Appreciation blooms, love's subtle arts,
Marking my essence, confidence a dream.

Each facet shines, a tapestry unique,
Authentic living, breathing vibrant hues.
Accepting gifts, joy and passion speak,
An opus of self, a tale that I strew.

To heal the wounds of yesteryears, I face,
With tenderness, the unveiled scars may mar.
Believing in potential, let dreams embrace,
A critic's voice subdued, a door ajar.

Self-awareness guides, a keen mind's eye,
Reflections unfold, truths I can't deny.
Insight and appreciation, never shy,
A stronger self emerges, reaching high.

I delve into depths, discover worth untold,
Embrace my being, a masterpiece of old.
Through self-recovery, treasures unfold,
A ballad of self-worth, a tale retold.

Critic's voice fades, gone,
Heart's role finds a unique path.
Bold, battle unfolds.

Critic's Saga

In the depths of my mind, a saga unfurls,
Where the critic's voice echoes and swirls.
Yet, resolute, I stand, my spirit un-swayed,
In the face of doubt, I won't be dismayed.

Through the web of self, distrust cascades,
A mesh of identity, where shadows are laid.
But within, a glimmer, a light in the haze,
I won't abandon myself in this complex maze.

Yearning to please, neglecting my own gaze,
Yet beneath the surface, a resilient blaze.
I won't abandon myself, the vow I uphold,
In the depths of my mind, where stories are told.

Self-remorse, heavy burdens to hold,
Yet rising above, my spirit unfolds.
In the depths of my mind, the battle takes flight,
Through self-compassion, I find solace and light.

Embracing my worth, recalling I'm whole,
The journey within, a reclamation of soul.
No longer captive to the critic's cold hold,
I find my unique path with a heart that's bold.

In the depths of my mind, where battles are rife,
I won't abandon myself, embracing my life.
For within, a fire, a force that's resilient,
A blaze that burns, unyielding and brilliant.

Through trials faced, this flame withstood,
The echoes of time, unwavering and good.
Accepting my truth, with flaws unmasked,
In the heart's sanctuary, a refuge amassed.

Gifts bring pure delight,
Your influence fuels foresight.
Grace in giving's light.

Key to Growth

To navigate life's intricate path with grace,
Acknowledge truths that find their steadfast place.
Live attuned to the rhythms your heart deems true,
Align with the substance that resonates with you.

Nested in you, a pre-birth objective's clear,
To discover joy, let your soul's expansion steer.
As life unfolds, priorities may rearrange,
Yet, on intention's path, essence won't estrange.

Changes may unfold, veering into the unknown,
Yet, each step you take is a rebirth of your own.
In every twist and turn, in life's grand convention,
Move in harmony with your pre-birth intention.

The gift you share with this collective domain,
It isn't found in tasks or material gain.
In possession's grip, don't stake your stance,
With creative flow, let your essence advance.

Purpose isn't amassed or clutched too tight,
But thrives in the joyous sharing of your light.
See not the act as loss or a dwindling supply,
Rather, a gain that lifts your spirit sky-high.

Discover a gift that brings you pure delight,
Contribution, the key to growth in life's foresight.
In giving, unearth a wellspring of boundless grace,
A treasure enriching your life's profound embrace.

Friend, confidant true,
Not just words, trust deeply sown.
Ally loyal, free.

Steadfast Ally

In every relationship, unseen current flows,
An exchange of energy, subtle and profound.
Some feel its dance, while others in repose,
Yet its existence persists, silent and unbound.

Love, a distinct realm, an intimate art,
To embrace another as part of one's own.
Compassion, understanding's a start,
In love's embrace, a shared spirit is sown.

Real love is to nurture, caring unfolds,
Harm to the cherished rebounds the heart.
To act against its interest, a tale untold,
Is hurting ourselves, our wounding starts.

A good exchange, a reciprocal art,
Each find in it something deeply prized.
Value emerges from the core of the heart,
Reflecting needs and wants harmonized.

To understand oneself is where it begins,
Desires, offerings, a relationship chart.
Recognizing limits, where each one grins,
Two energy types, a nuanced part.

In knowing needs and wants, the key,
For in the depths of self, Divine love does dwell.
Compatibility assessed, love's symphony,
The most intimate bond, we ever shall tell.

Contract of self-love,
Promising presence and care.
Ignite eternal fires.

Eternal Fire

In realms of billions, I stand alone,
A voyage through depths uniquely my own.
No kinship forged can fathom or defend,
The symphony where hopes and fears blend.

Oh, I'm a melody, unheard, unseen,
In realms untrodden, where I convene.
A sacred vow to cradle my own heart,
Life's canvas painted, a masterful art.

In wedded words, solemn oaths we weave,
Yet do we pledge ourselves, believe?
To tend and nurture, through night and day,
In self-love's covenant, come what may.

Within this pact of care and self-esteem,
I promise to endure, in joy and dream.
To honor needs, desires that transpire,
Igniting my soul's eternal fire.

So let us stand tall, commit to our song,
A pact with ourselves, where we belong.
Amongst the multitude, find our own worth,
Accepting our essence, restored New Earth.

Self-care blooms anew,
Prioritize well-being,
Wisdom's depths unveiled.

POWERFUL BOND

To build a bond with oneself, so true,
A lonely path of self-discovery anew.
Here are some thoughts, a humble reflection,
On fostering self's vital connection.

Embrace life's experience, don't repeat,
The recurrences should not deplete.
In the humdrum, find beauty's hidden bloom,
Discovering depth, beyond the outer gloom.

Unveil new perspectives, a fresh open lens,
Innovate thoughts, where growth extends.
Challenge the norms, the patterns well-known,
Expand horizons, where true self is shown.

Nurture the mundane, for it holds treasures,
In ordinary moments, find life's measures.
Accept simplicity, let it play its part,
For within its rhythm lies a beating heart.

Listen to the whispers of your own soul,
In stillness, truth and wisdom will unroll.
Acknowledge needs and aspirations,
Ignite the fires of gnosis and revelations.

With each passing moment, let self-care thrive,
Prioritize your well-being, truly alive.
Inside the conga of spirit, a constant reprise,
Of universal truth where intelligence lies.

So, embark on this journey, steadfast and bold,
Forge a bond with yourself, as the days unfold.
A good relationship begins with you taking heed,
An honest endeavor, the soul's noble creed.

Relationship's grace,
Transformative dance unfolds,
Sow self-awareness.

Seeds of Intention

In the garden of self, with mindful intention,
I sow seeds of awareness, a lifelong ascension.
A journey unfolds, each chapter untold,
Moving closer to a cherished sensation.

With committed goals, overarching and grand,
Each passing year, a story in my hand.
Consciously sowing, the seeds take root,
A dance with time, a personal pursuit.

As seasons change, in mindful adaptation,
Embracing shifts with quiet anticipation.
Closer to self, with each ebb and flow,
A cherished embrace, a continuous glow.

Through highs and lows, joy, and distress,
The path may meander, a maze to impress.
Yet boldly I walk, with purpose in the air,
Sowing seeds of self, with an unwavering stare.

To thrive and evolve, I assess and grow,
Life's tapestry unfolding, a rhythmic flow.
Moving ever closer, with each passing trace,
To a cherished heart, a harmonious space.

Self-relationship is key to finesse,
A change groovy, in the heart's recess.
Sowing purpose, like seeds in the land,
Moving closer to my inner Divine, hand in hand.

In the garden of self, with mindful intention,
I sow seeds of awareness, a lifelong ascension.
A journey unfolds, each chapter untold,
Moving closer to a cherished sensation.

Reject not, but feel,
Anger, sadness, fear arise.
Acknowledge with peace.

Art of Healing

Inside my feelings, I tread with care,
A ballad of suffering, let me share.
Anger, sadness, and fear, they reside,
A swirl of emotions, where hearts collide.

Anxiety and panic, they loom near,
When I deny feelings, what I most fear.
Yet emotions are genuine and pure,
It's my thoughts that obscure their allure.

In the throes of anger, relationships strain,
A daunting challenge, emotions in disdain.
Feelings of powerlessness, a source of strife,
Causing pain, a threat, complicating life.

In moments of fear, in the clasp of hurt's hand,
Anger emerges, a weight hard to withstand.
A signal, a reflex, a self-preserving chase,
A response to regain a sense of grace.

It springs from a core of perceived defeat,
A longing for control, a force replete.
To navigate this tempest, a conscious start,
I transform the impulse, a mindful part.

In the crucible of anger, mastery unfolds,
Control is not in suppression, wisdom it holds.
If unprocessed, emotions grow,
A torrential storm, an inner woe.

No longer suppressed, I set them free,
Open, vulnerable, let them be.
To heal my heart, I must be bold,
Address, clear, let emotions unfold.

Let suffering cease, and peace shall start,
It's the art of healing, a hymn from the heart.

Acceptance's guide,
Riding life's tides, high and low,
Curiosity's stride.

Curiosity Blooms

My inner journey of self, let curiosity bloom,
Embracing the winds of change, let them entwine.
Uncertainty's veil may cast a fleeting gloom,
But through it, new growth pathways we find.

With acceptance as our steadfast guide,
We ride the tides of life, their highs and lows.
In transformations, we courageously stride,
Emerging from struggles, wisdom in our throes.

Amidst the waves that crash upon our shore,
A stable core emerges, strong and true.
Defining our essence, forevermore,
A foundation cherished, authentic and blue.

In the journey of self, let us embrace,
Curiosity and acceptance, with love's grace.

Sickness whispers soft,
Seeking attention, it speaks.
Balance holds the key.

Body's Messengers

Within our human bodies, secret codes hide,
A drapery of wonders, yearning to be untied.
An orchestra of cells, entwined with grace,
A dance of unity, every part finds its place.

Yet toxins, vile intruders, upset this sacred dance,
Bringing imbalance, a disruptor's chance.
An intricate web of connections, unstable, frayed,
A signal, a warning, our intelligent system conveyed.

Conflicts within, a battle waged beneath our skin,
Cravings for sweetness, addiction's tempting din.
Anxiety's grip and blame that stains our souls,
These imbalances arise, as our body's bell tolls.

For when sickness knocks, a messenger it be,
Seeking our attention, longing for our decree.
In the ebb and flow of giving and receiving,
Lies the path to health, the secret to believing.

In the art of balance, there's an opus for mercy,
Nurture this inner clarity, without controversy.
With mindful choices, we can heal and restore,
Optimal well-being, a state worth striving for.

So let us listen closely to the whispers from within,
Embrace the hidden truths, the journey begins.
For the human body holds mysteries untold,
A ballad of life's messages, waiting to unfold.

Building blocks of care,
Connecting body and soul,
Nurturing each day.

Pillars of Care

In the realm of self-care, let's commence,
Prioritizing the foundations strong,
Sleep, nutrition, activity immense,
Rest, recreation, this is where I belong.

These building blocks, the pillars of care,
Connects me with my body, spirit bright,
Being custodian, aware and fair,
Nurturing holistically, day and night.

For physical needs, the key to thrive,
Supporting all aspects of life's design,
A testament on how to truly strive,
To cherish our innocence and align.

Mental habits, behaviors to refine,
Nourished by self-care, our souls enshrine.

Self-love's gentle path,
Kindness guides appraisal's flow.
No harsh criticism.

Gentle Empathy

On the path of self-love, let kindness reside,
A gentle approach to how we confide.
No need for harsh criticism's cruel blow,
Instead, appraise with a caring flow.

Blame may arise, but let it not control,
For the excessive critic may take its toll.
Accept what comes, but with a gentle touch,
Not off the hook, responsibility we clutch.

Be candid, yet compassionate and caring,
In self-review, there's balance we're recovering.
No need to let aggression take its place,
Take responsibility with a tender grace.

In the realm of self, let kindness be the key,
Balancing appraisal with gentle empathy.

One goal every day,

Windfall flows, accomplishments.

Small steps, satisfaction.

Achievable Goals

In the pursuit of change, let optimism grow,
Yet realism is the guiding light we see,
Perfectionism, its destructive force we know,
All-or-nothing thinking, let it be set free.

Short-term fixes, a tempting siren's call,
Often leading to failure's bitter sting,
Self-blame's cycle, maintaining its thrall,
Cracking the whip, no solace does it bring.

Beware the dark path of self-abuse and pain,
Not a recipe for change, healthy and sound,
Though maladaptive defenses we may explain,
Clutching too tightly, growth cannot be found.

Frustration, a catalyst for transformation,
Setting achievable goals, a wise foundation.

Craft a crisis plan,

Embrace support, find solace.

Vulnerability.

Moments of Solace

In moments dire, a plan my heart does mold,
Through life's tumult, both new and old.
Regrets may haunt, yet bravely I face,
Embracing vulnerability in life's race.

Old habits, like shadows, may try to sway,
But strength and foresight hold them at bay.
In written thoughts, a lifeline I trace,
A soothing balm for my soul's fierce pace.

In kin's support, a comforting balm,
Their wisdom, a shield, in life's stormy qualm.
I embrace their help, let connections grow,
For in unity's hold, true strengths doth show.

Through life's tapestry, stressors may weave,
Roles entwine, hearts hoping to believe.
Change, a constant, whispers in my ear,
A mutation, unknown path that's unclear.

In marriage's grasp, loneliness may dwell,
Yet in shared solitude, our hearts often swell.
Crisis reveals, identity reborn,
A phoenix rising from shadows torn.

The empty nest echoes with memories sweet,
A cycle of love, in the family's heartbeat.
Death leaves a stain, but life's threads persist,
A caregiver's journey, love's tender tryst.

In life's mosaic, each piece has a role,
Love, loss, and grace, interwoven and whole.
This sonnet of existence, a timeless trace,
A narrative spun with love's tender grace.

Meaningful actions,
Life's symphony in motion,
My integrity.

Integrity Preserved

On the path to fulfilling our life's song,
I maintain meaningful activity, all day long.
Success, not stagnant, but in actions I find,
Fulfillment and accomplishment, intertwined.

Work, though not always a job I adore,
I seek ways to make it significant and more.
Whether a change in tasks or perspective's gaze,
Integrity and purpose, a job's profound ablaze.

Beyond work's domain, I seek joy in stride,
Hobbies, recreation, and time by my side.
In service to others, giving back to my core,
Meaningful bonds, love's treasure to explore.

But I don't forget, in my own mind I dwell,
A source of appeal, I have more stories to tell.
I nurture my thoughts, find entertainment anew,
In self-discovery, a world to pursue.

Intentions held close,
Guide our actions, shape our path,
Goals bloom with each step.

ORMING GOOD HABITS

Let's wake up with purpose, set our path anew,
Establish our habits, strong and ever true.
To foster self-relationship goals we seek,
Begin our day in ways that we can keep.

It may be helpful, penning goals at night,
To greet the morn with visions clear and bright.
While I like to hold intentions with my mind,
A mental map of how my day will unwind.

No matter how we choose to start each morn,
Let's remind ourselves of what we truly yearn.
Our visions and dreams, let them take flight,
Review key practices in morning's light.

We prepare to face the challenges ahead,
With clarity, rehearse our steps to tread.
Though spontaneity has its own grace,
We keep goals in mind, guiding each pace.

For when we live with purpose in our hearts,
Our actions align, each piece plays its part.
So let each dawn awaken with resolve,
To shape our days, and with intent evolve.

Feel your heart's rhythm,
Agitation's fiery grip,
Calmness brings relief.

Self-Talk's Tone

Beware of harsh self-talk, a cautionary tale,
Where bitter words echo, hearts begin to wail.
When we catch ourselves speaking cruel and loud,
It's time to pause, step back from the shroud.

Take a moment to feel our heart's wild beat,
Are we agitated? Do we feel the heat?
Criticism flows fast, like a raging river,
But in this reflection, let kindness deliver.

Slow down our speech, with calmness and care,
Embrace tranquility, let our soul repair.
Reassess the situation with a peaceful view,
And when ready, try again, with purpose anew.

We can find solace in conversations out loud,
Finding our voice, beneath the stars' proud shroud.
Under the right conditions, this can truly aid,
In finding clarity, where answers are laid.

So, remember, when self-talk takes a bitter tone,
Interrupt the action, with a kinder pitch to own.
Reflect, recalibrate, let understanding grow,
In the realm of self-talk, let compassion show.

Self-love's gentle breeze,

Nurtures bonds, lets love take flight,

Trust blooms, songs ignite.

Wings Aloft

Self-love reigns, a vital refrain,
The cornerstone of bonds we treasure.
With wings aloft, love's song sustain.

In every heart, its power remains,
Nurturing ties, a lasting measure.
Self-love reigns, a vital refrain.

Embrace its breath, let not self-doubt constrain,
It's the foundation of every pleasure.
With wings aloft, love's song sustain.

A symphony of trust, free from strain,
With self-compassion as our treasure,
Self-love reigns, a vital refrain.

Through highs and lows, it will maintain,
A balm for wounds, a source of leisure.
With wings aloft, love's song sustain.

In all relationships, let's not abstain,
From cherishing ourselves without measure.
Self-love reigns, a vital refrain,
With wings aloft, love's song sustain.

Colors hold the key,
Revealing consciousness depths,
Truth luminescent.

SPECTRUM OF COLORS

Within the spectrum of colors we find,
A glimpse into the depths of consciousness,
Reincarnation's cycle intertwined,
Revealing shades of luminescence.

Seven densities, each with its own grace,
Unfolding realms as we ascend and grow,
Through unity and oneness, we embrace,
Transcending limitations, we will know.

In service to others, our purpose lies,
Expanding our awareness, reaching higher,
Evolving souls, ascending to the skies,
In an energetic match, we will aspire.

The tapestry of life, with colors bright,
Guides our spiritual evolution's flight.

Canvas unfurls wide,
Divine potential takes hold,
Story to unfold.

True Destiny

In human form, a sacred path we tread,
Divine-self moving through time's thread,
The veil of forgetting, a necessary rite,
Embodied in form, to shine divine light.

Here, self-actualization finds its space,
Planet Earth, our vessel, our destined place,
Full potential realized, manifested clear,
Life's lessons and experiences draw near.

Through trials and triumphs, we come to see,
The depths of our being, our true destiny,
A canvas to demonstrate, to unfold,
Divine potential, a story to be told.

So let us honor this sacred incarnation,
Embrace the journey, with divine dedication,
For in this realm, our purpose we unveil,
A testament to love, as we live and prevail.

Contradictions stir,
Fighting reality's weight.
Oneness, truth's embrace.

Reality's Mercy

Oneness, the highest truth of the universe,
Alignment brings harmony, peace to unfold,
Suffering fades as love becomes our nurse.

When contradictions arise, life's adverse,
Fighting reality, a tale yet untold,
Oneness, the highest truth of the universe.

Reality's mercy, a wake-up call, a verse,
To change our perception, a story to mold,
Suffering fades as love becomes our nurse.

Divine human self, in love we immerse,
Embracing the unity, a bond to uphold,
Oneness, the highest truth of the universe.

Love, our guiding star, with blessings diverse,
Leading us towards a harmonious threshold,
Suffering fades as love becomes our nurse.

In these relations of life, let love disperse,
For in Oneness, our spirits are consoled,
Oneness, the highest truth of the universe,
Suffering fades as love becomes our nurse.

Freedom in focus,
Awakening self, love's path,
Shedding chains of fear.

Upleveling Soul

Freedom blooms when attention finds its place,
In truth, empowering hearts to soar with grace.
Expanding self-awareness, we uplevel,
Detoxifying souls, embracing love's revel.

To heal and love our neighbors, we're aligned,
Negativity's grip we leave behind.
For in the artificial matrix, we're bound,
In hate, fear, manipulation profound.

Deception, wars, confusion's tangled plight,
Worry chains constrict, restricting our light.
But we can choose a different path to tread,
Where freedom reigns, love's essence is spread.

With focused minds on gratitude dwell,
Breaking the chains, in truth, we will excel.

Sacred flow rings true,

Choice yours, in all you pursue.

Gift profound, unbound.

SACRED UNION

The physical density, tales are spun,
Of currency potent, when day is done.
Sexual energy, precious and rare,
A power to shape, an affair to share.

Some spend it freely, on lust's desire,
Chasing pleasure, consumed by the fire.
But in this path, a descent they find,
Leaving their spirit and growth behind.

Yet those who choose wisely with grace,
Save this energy for a higher embrace.
Divine Union awaits, a love so deep,
Ascending swiftly, their souls do leap.

This currency, a key to transformation,
Nervous system upgraded in elation.
A blissful existence, a state unknown,
As this energy builds, they've truly grown.

We learn that the sacred flow rings true,
The choice is yours, in all that you do.
With sexual energy, a gift profound,
May you journey to heights unbound.

Generate stargate,
Act with love and devotion,
Gifting thyself peace.

Action is Key

In the depths of my stargate, a treasure,
A fount of wisdom, where secrets reside,
Dharma's essence, like honeyed nectar's measure,
A source of truth, where love's grace does preside.

With each dawn, my soul embraces the light,
Gratefulness fills my heart, I take a sip,
Cosmic wisdom flows, pure and bright,
A sacred elixir, a divine trip.

In pursuit of the state of desired Being,
I unlock truth, the key is action's might,
With devotion's grace, my vision's foreseeing,
Love overflows, a celestial flight.

My heart bursts with boundless affection,
Embodying the green ray's divine connection,
A gift of peace, my soul's sweet reflection,
A perfect energy exchange, love's perfection.

Igniting flames within, my heart's own fire,
The daily gift that fuels my soul's desire,
Through the green portal, my spirit flies higher,
An offering to all, my essence set to aspire.

Soul rises, time's height,
Ego's journey spans in width.
Love transcends it all.

VERTICAL PATH

The soul, a vertical voyage it takes,
While ego's journey moves on the horizontal plane.
In timeliness, the heart's true love awakes,
Effortless, pouring out, ceaseless rain.

With trust and forgiveness fully embraced,
Escaping time's grasp, ascending above.
A spiraling ascent, no longer encased,
Into eternity's realm, a flight is like a dove.

Time, a mere measure, linear and grand,
Guiding our learning, in this earthly quest.
Moments woven in life's intricate strand,
The soul flutters, time's partner, ever blessed.

Let us embrace both realms, intertwined,
In this sonnet of time, our spirits aligned.

Densities unfold,
Light reveals boundless brilliance.
Universe's hymn.

STAGES OF EVOLUTION

Consciousness unfolds through seven densities,
Evolution's stages, progressing with ease.
Light, the substance that shapes reality's flow,
Empowers awareness and wisdom to bestow.

As density increases, more light is found,
Information, expression, brilliance unbound.
Through the Universe, light's the sole medium,
Manifesting perception, its cosmic anthem.

In the third density, our planet's quest,
A crucial transition, to choose and invest.
Polarity's decision, each level's graduation,
An opportunity for growth and elevation.

When awareness aligns with heart's radiant glow,
Photon light within us, our planet's frequency grows.
Bound by destiny, a collective endeavor,
In service to one another, united forever.

Consciousness rises,
Embrace the limitless self.
Fearless lion heart.

Lion Hearts

The rise of awareness, a sacred test,
To embrace our limitless nature, blessed.
Not merely shedding false layers in flight,
But embodying our higher self's pure light.

Eternal beings, fleeting mortal days,
Life's brevity is a chance for soul's embrace.
The magnitude immense, our higher self's call,
Countless lifetimes, the soul's grand hall.

With courage, we unveil the truth within,
No more playing small, let greatness begin.
Cultivate lion-hearts, roar with pride and might,
Accepting the I AM presence, infinite sight.

In this journey, let our souls ignite,
Embracing truth, ascending to new heights.

Unchanging being,
Divine essence, no facade,
Illusions released.

Illusions Fade

Life persists, regardless of thought,
Belief holds sway, discord naught.
Happiness springs from inner conviction,
Truth reigns supreme, in every depiction.

Our being, constant perfection's embrace,
Divine essence within, with no trace,
Illusion dissolves, as we honor and allow,
Denial and resistance, we disavow.

The awakened mind, serene and composed,
Graceful and humble, in each moment exposed.
Embracing the presence, experience's delight,
In quietude, finding wisdom's insightful light.

For in the depths of truth, illusions fade,
The awakened soul, in harmony, is laid.

Waves within the sea,
Reflect our interconnectedness,
Sky before clouds.

Boundless and Free

In search of truth's key, do we yearn to be free?
Or are we already boundless, forever decree?
From dreams we awaken, to realities vast,
For freedom resides in each moment's contrast.

No external realm holds our true liberation,
Within rests the mirror, our self-reflection.
The universe echoes our inner state of being,
Love and purity, the lens we are seeing.

As waves are to the ocean, so are we to all,
Source of existence, where our spirits enthrall.
The sky precedes clouds, its vastness supreme,
Likewise, the feeler precedes the feeling's gleam.

Thoughts arise, but the thinker is the root,
Greater than the concepts, in wisdom's pursuit.
Manifestations form with the observer's might,
Greater still, the source of creation's pure light.

We are the fullness, the essence of the Divine,
The Light of the world, in our hearts it shines.
Desires lie within, present here and now,
Embracing our truth, with gratitude we bow.

Light-filled mind at peace,
Fear fades like raindrops on glass.
Innocence restored.

Infinite Peace

A mind adorned with grace finds tranquil ease,
Fear's grip no longer disturbs its peace.
A ghostly presence, fleeting and transient,
As light within dawns, fears become distant.

Like raindrops on a windshield's surface fleeting,
They cannot steer our vision's steady meeting.
For healing isn't found in changing who we are,
But in recalling the child's innocence, pure and far.

Free, infinite, flawless, our inner essence shines,
Embracing our truth, where divinity aligns.
No longer burdened by fear's weighty plight,
We journey forward on the path of light.

In harmony we dwell, enjoying each day,
Fear dissolves, as light guides our way.
Remembering our nature, pure and free,
Our true selves awaken, eternally.

Rainbow buds brightly,
Unfettered by surface tides.
Pure eyes find true light.

True Colours

In the depths of stillness, hidden away,
Lies a gift of grandeur, for us to convey.
Accepting the now, breaking the chains,
A cycle shattered, freedom surely remains.

Within the silence, a treasure untold,
Showing mysteries that time can't withhold.
The eternal nature, a wondrous sight,
Unveiling the enigma, both day and night.

We are the seekers, liberated and free,
Like a lotus arising from murky debris.
Life's cycles expanding, grace unwinds,
Releasing illusions, true colors we find.

A world of beauty, like a rainbow in bloom,
Not imposed by currents, we rise and assume.
Softening our gaze, turning inward our sight,
Pure eyes behold us, bathed in radiant light.

So let this verse echo with a heartfelt tune,
Of stillness like the sweetest lagoon.
Let's choose to embrace the treasure true,
A tale of awakening where our spirits renew.

Center's sacred touch,
Harmony's thread interweaves,
Love's divine embrace.

Magic Interlaced

In realms unseen, where mysteries reside,
Our minds perceive, rhythmic sway they glide.
A complex orchestra, our brain's refrain,
Translating reality's enigmatic domain.

What seems so solid, a glowing masquerade,
Energies vibrate in melodical cascade.
Our eyes glimpse the effulge subtle and grand,
As forms take shape at our command.

Pulsating waves connect us, heart to heart,
A symphony of light, where unity imparts.
Within this cosmic embroidery we're bound,
A multiverse of wonders, waiting to be found.

Yet, observer's gaze holds power untold,
As quantum threads of truth, together they unfold.
In space, in time, and objects that we perceive,
A harmony's woven, an intricate reprieve.

To our center, let us journey and explore,
Where love's divine essence forever does endure.
In this harmonious thread, we're embraced,
Connected to all, love's magic interlaced.

Shadows crave the light,
Existence bound to its glow.
Light shines on its own.

Light's Shadow

In the dance of luminescence and gloom,
A shadow emerges, a tender loom,
When light's path, halted by object's might,
Darkness follows, a veil in the night.

With reliance on light, shadows find their form,
Cast by the radiance, they quietly swarm,
No light, no shadows, a truth we concede,
For darkness crumbles when light takes the lead.

But light codes of data is a divine force,
Unfettered by darkness, it takes its course,
It bathes the world in its glorious gleam,
Unfazed by the absence of shadows' theme.

Electromagnetic waves, in dazzling flight,
Through space they travel, in brilliance alight,
Matter they touch, they interact and play,
Perceiving the world in their vibrant display.

Thus shadows, they crave the light,
To exist, they require its gleaming might,
Yet light, self-assured, can illuminate alone,
With or without darkness, its radiance shown.

So let shadows dance, and let them play,
For light's rhythm guides them, day by day,
In this intricate symphony, they find their place,
While light, ever glorious, casts its eternal grace.

Midlife's stage, a plea,
Soul seeks truth, essence set free.
Odyssey's decree.

Crisis of the Soul

Upon this stage of life, my soul does cry,
A yearning deep within, a crisis near,
No mere upheaval, but a heartfelt sigh,
In search of truth, my essence to endear.

Navigating midlife's uncharted sea,
No crisis, but a quest for self so true,
A rediscovery, the soul set free,
In life's rich tapestry, a vibrant hue.

The chapters written in the book of years,
Reveal a yearning for authenticity,
A profound cry, dispelling inner fears,
The quest for self, a sacred odyssey.

Oh, let this soul discharge its authentic plea,
In midlife's change, my true essence sees.

Navigating Change

Hormones shift and change,
Perimenopause whispers.
Farewell to the flow.

Time's passage unveils,
Perimenopause tale unknown,
Estrogen's farewell.

Shifting Symphony

In the passage of time, a journey unfolds,
Perimenopause, a tale yet untold.
Ovaries once vibrant, now yield their hold,
As estrogen's clench gradually grows cold.

A tissue's creation, through veins it'll flow,
To bring about change, physiological show.
Each month a surprise, an unstable spree,
Within the chaos, deeper meanings to see.

In the realm of transition, my body embarked,
Atypical menses where the path grew arched.
Baking hot and chilling cold, a fading display,
Less hormones produced, a sequence astray.

In a rhythmic cadence, my body would sway,
A finale to creation, where fertility may stray.
Estrogen's decline and hormones askew,
As testosterone surges, a molten rave ensues.

Ever-changing tides,
Hormones may produce chaos.
Strength blooms in the storm.

Changing Tides

Like the changing tides, we ebb and flow,
A testament to nature's cyclical show,
With courage, women embrace the unknown,
Navigating the waters we have sown.

Hormonal whispers lead with a subtle hand,
A transformative path, both intricate and grand.
Irregular periods, the clue to life's demand,
Reminding us of our strength as we withstand.

Ovulation's murmur, once steady and true,
Now disrupted, in disarray and in queue.
Estrogen and progesterone, a duo so grand,
Guiding ovulation and cycles by hand.

Fluctuating levels, like a rollercoaster ride,
Transition's journey where emotions collide.
Up and down, the hormones would glide,
A wild trot of changes, with no place to hide.

Oh, the ebb and flow, the rise and fall,
Menopause at the door, a hormonal call.
Like waves crashing upon the shore,
Our body's symphony, forevermore.

Fiery blooms ignite,
Hot flashes flood cheeks in light.
Resilience takes flight.

Fiery Blooms

Hot flashes, fiery blooms of heat,
A flame that engulfs, from head to feet,
Cheeks ablaze, a sensation so fleet,
Yet in their wake, a cadence of heartbeat.

Oh, menopause, a journey of change,
Embracing the inferno, no need to estrange.
For in the fire, resilience shall reign,
A retreat within, where power shall remain.

From internal depth, a furnace ignites,
A surge of warmth on unexpected nights.
Skin aflame, the body takes flight,
Yet I stand strong with the newfound light.

Cheeks flushed with hues of pink and red,
The flames of alteration, no need to dread.
A reminder of life's blaze, boldly spread,
The tribute to strength in which I tread.

In the dance of heat, I strip and find release,
A transformation, bringing inner peace.
Each flash is a reminder that I am fierce,
Resilience, my sanctuary, never to cease.

Oh, menopause, a journey of change,
Embracing the heat, no need to estrange,
For in the fire, resilience shall reign,
A retreat, within, where power shall remain.

Nocturnal sweats,
Dampened sheets, moonlit embrace.
Dreams carry solace.

Nocturnal Affair

In the realm of night, perspiration's cry,
Beneath the moonlit sky, a clammy sigh.
Amidst damp linens, I wake and ponder why,
In slumber's embrace, the longest night's sigh.

With rest's gentle sway by sleep disturbed,
Insomnia's unwelcome presence curbed.
Yet I persevere, longing for inertia's light,
Embracing the darkness, hugging its might.

Oh, menopause, this nocturnal affair,
A rumba of sweat, a burden hard to bear.
But in the clinging moisture, resilience thrives,
Through the darkest hours, my spirit revives.

In twilight hours, I find sweet reprieve,
'Midst clinging moistness, solace I receive.
For in my dreams, a sanctuary revealed,
A sacred space where my soul is unsealed.

Night sweats, faithful mates they've become,
Though moisture reigns, my rest won't be undone.
With dreams as refuge, blessed I'll ever be,
Embracing the respite, my spirit flies free.

Emotions in salsa,
Mood swings kaleidoscope spins.
Devotion that guides.

Swinging Moods

Within this journey, emotions twirl,
Mood swings, a web ever unfurled.
Irritability, anxiety, tumultuous whirl,
Devotion guides us facing life's hurl.

The yoni's drought, a reminder so tender,
To nurture intimacy, our love we render.
Exploring with open hearts in surrender,
Self-love's clasp, feelings shall engender.

Menopause, a challenge to our desire,
Libido's flame may flicker, momentarily tire.
But desire endures, the spark won't expire,
Love's fervent pyre burns with passion's fire.

Sensual urges, a tempo unsteady,
Yearning flickers, passion holds steady.
With softness and unwavering patience,
We'll conquer this arid phase with brilliance.

So let this verse echo far and wide,
In this hormonal tale, we shall not hide.
With coherent moods and prism inside,
Sharing our stories, as life takes its stride.

Body's change brings woes,
Urinary troubles rise,
Muscle function wanes.

BLADDER'S CONTROL

In this stage of life, experiences unfold,
Impacting bladder's hold, a truth to be told.
Questions arise as functions seem to wane,
Clarity needed amidst this hormonal reign.

Urinary troubles surface, a call-in need,
Estrogen's absence, bladder's plea to heed.
Frequent leakage, urgency's command,
Embarrassment buzzes, loss hard to withstand.

Menopause's touch unveils challenges anew,
Flow's transformation, a different view.
Heavier or lighter, the pattern takes shape,
No shame in asking for help, a brief escape.

Spotting between cycles, an unexpected stain,
A gentle reminder of our body's refrain.
With vesica function under construction,
Seek pelvic floor treatments, follow instructions.

As bodies change, courage leads the way,
Navigating shifts with strength every day.
Frequent tinkling, nature's demanding call,
Together we rise to meet it all.

As we navigate this path, challenges arise,
This phase is hidden behind a clever guise.
Yet in the depth of change, we stand tall,
Finding grace and vigor, overcoming it all.

In silence we tread,
Menopause's a lonely quest.
Shame's judgment persists.

Lonely Quest

Years after my hysterectomy,
I battled insomnia, sadness, fatigue.
Unexplained weight gain, zero memory,
Frequent tears, a storm inside of me.

In the hospital with chest pain I lay,
Juggling much, health's decline at play.
Foggy brain, forgetfulness enshroud,
Feeling like I'm losing it, a disarray.

With humiliation, my frustration in tow,
Negative thoughts arise, moments of woe.
Obvious events forgotten, a family jest,
All connected to menopause, lack of flow.

Navigating this change is a lonely quest,
No one speaks about their mental health.
We struggle isolated, avoiding the stigma,
The shame of silence and verdict's clear.

Are they only hot flashes or something more?
Menopause's trace, a connection I explore.
The puzzle pieces align, a clearer view,
My body's journey of changes I can't ignore.

Within the depths of extreme hormonal sway,
I mourn the woman I was, day by day.
Yet in this elegy, a glimmering truth,
I am not alone in this evolutionary couth.

Let us shed the shroud of silence and shame,
Illuminate the path with empathy's flame.
In remembrance of our true nature, we flee,
United in this heroic journey, we shall see.

Fading light reflects,
Weight gained in endless struggle.
Knee whispers of time.

Weight of Change

Eyesight dims, light fades, twilight's descent,
Weight gained in strife, a fight without end.
My knee, a trusted guide, aged and wise,
Over time, my creaky bone signs arise.

In this transition, youth mourned, I weep,
Each day a dirge, memories buried deep.
Yet truth takes wing in this sonnet's embrace,
Kinship's light's found in transformative grace.

High and low I searched, solace to retrieve,
Paths exhausted, seeking a cure, I believe.
Through exercise's trials, strength I'd ignite,
Nourishing my body, meals chosen right.

Supplements consumed, hoping for respite,
Prayers whispered, reaching beyond the night.
Meditation's solace, calming my restless mind,
With gentle massages, tensions aligned.

Medication tried, prescribed with care,
Yearning for relief from the burdens I bear.
But amidst my efforts, still I quest,
A remedy unknown, unique at its behest.

On this winding journey, I wander and roam,
Exploring new realms, combing what's shown.
For answers may lie beyond my known sphere,
A healing poem awaiting, ready to appear.

Breaking silent chains,

Menopause's power shines.

Accept, invest, rise.

Shattering Taboos

In a world of whispers, a hush fills the air,
A subject taboo, a silence unfair.
Menopause, elusive and shamed,
Hesitant lips, their mention defamed.

Societal stigmas, judgments that loom,
Women keep quiet, concealing their gloom.
Fearful of reactions, the eyes that might gaze,
They hid in the shadows, trapped in a maze.

But breaking the silence, a daring stand,
Empowering voices united we expand.
For this change is natural, a part of life's tide,
It's time to educate, to cast disgrace aside.

Let's shed ignorance with understanding,
Lift the veil of stigma, with knowledge expanding.
Women's stories shared, our experiences heard,
No longer suppressed, our tones unstirred.

This golden journey is a chapter untold,
With care and support, hearts can unfold.
Together we'll rise, breaking the chains,
Receiving the power that life's change sustains.

No longer quiet, but with strength and pride,
We'll salvage the narrative, our truths abide.
A woman's story, we'll rewrite and reclaim,
Shattering taboos, in unity we proclaim.

Unveiling the truth,

Shedding the weight of judgment.

A liberation.

LEGENDS UNTOLD

In women's bodies, legends reside, untold,
From childbirth's marvel to the vibrant flow,
Menopause's arrival, a story to behold.

Within the chambers, a fiery grace unfolds,
Amidst the doubts that cast their shadows low,
In women's bodies, legends reside, untold.

Shame and silence, in past they've controlled,
But now we break the chains, let veracity glow,
Menopause's arrival, a story to behold.

A gilded chapter as life's seasons enfold,
Transforming rhythm, as nature wills it so,
In women's bodies, legends reside, untold,

Embrace the shifts, let wisdom's wings unfold,
Through education, empowerment will grow,
Menopause's arrival, a story to behold.

With a new narrative, let freedom be extolled,
No longer whispered, but with voices in tow,
In women's bodies, legends reside, untold,
Menopause's arrival, a story to behold.

Nourish energies,

Physical, Emotional,

Share with utmost care.

Nourishing Realms

In a world of haste and constant chase,
We must heed the call of deep fatigue.
Accustomed to a life of low pace,
Yet unaware of its risk unseen.

Physical vigor, a vital foundation,
Sleep, exercise, and nature's embrace.
Fresh air, pure water, our restoration,
Renewing strength, as time we embrace.

Emotional bonds, profound and true,
In love, family, and nature's grace.
Connection deep, hearts beating as two,
A refuge found in this cherished space.

Cognitive growth, a journey untold,
In learning's realm, our minds ignite.
Intellectual flames, they never fold,
A fire within, burning bright.

Spiritual essence, a sacred call,
Through meditation's serene domain.
The quest for purpose, a path for all,
In soulful realms, we shall regain.

Social connections, bonds that mend,
In friends and community's warm embrace.
Workdays shared, together we blend,
In person, we find our cherished place.

For in the ballad of life's sweet tune,
We must nourish each note with care.
Harmonizing the energies strewn,
To thrive and flourish everywhere.

Empowered voices,
Shattering taboos of shame,
Secrets revealed.

Hushed Whispers

In hushed confessions, secrets tightly clasp,
A veil of shame society doth weave,
A chorus echoes taboo, shadows grasp.

Unspoken tales, in shades they deceive,
Dismissed, ignored, the cycle bears its strife,
In whispered tones, secrets tightly cleave.

Yet winds of change breathe whispers into life,
Empowering all, breaking silence's chain,
A chorus sings of truth, cutting through the strife.

No longer veiled, the heart is free from pain,
Taboos shattered, understanding takes flight,
In quiet tones, secrets break the strain.

With knowledge and care, we mend the night,
Compassion blooms, hearts pulsing to the sound,
A chorus sings of love, its power bright.

Menopause embraced, pride stands unbound,
No more confined by society's cruel game,
In hushed whispers, secrets now are crowned,
A chorus sings of strength, its power aflame.

Media's cruel gaze,
Distorts truth with its harsh glare.
Shame fills the airwaves.

Dispelling Myths

The media spins views, myths intertwine,
Causing distress, facts are harder to define.
They cast a cloud upon our weary minds,
But we'll break free, falsehoods left behind.

Let truth shine, revealing what's real,
Expose the folklore, with clarity we deal.
Hormonal balance guides on new paths,
By choice reclaimed, no longer a wrath.

We're not alone in this tumultuous ride,
Solutions exist, empowering our stride.
In the bedroom, transformations unfold,
Game-changers arise, our stories are told.

Estrogen's samba affects our frame,
Fat finds refuge from life's harsh game.
Around the waist, hips, thighs, it resides,
Yet self-love blooms, doubts subside.

No need to suffer, endure a cruel plight,
Relief is warranted, no apologies in sight.
Seeking vitality and health, our spirits rise,
Embracing freedom, defiantly wise.

This change beckons us to delve within,
Rediscover passions, let desire begin.
Menopause's path, an occasion grand,
To reignite desire, life's pleasure gland.

Monthly tide's end,
Bloating and headaches subside,
A calmness prevails.

Unique Path

I challenge the tales that bind and restrict,
The story that we must not contradict.
An experience varied, unique paths linked,
In this transition, new discoveries are distinct.

For me, it's freedom, a time to thrive,
To spread my wings, accept life's vibrant hive.
With goodwill and caring, self-love reigns,
This change has become a gift to sustain.

Liberation beckons, a chance to soar,
I welcome the changes like never before.
With self-care and grace, I'll find my way,
Menopause's sonnet, let it sing and play.

No more worries about the monthly tide,
Bloating and headaches, they now subside.
Peace reigns within, calmness prevails,
In this beauty of change, our spirit sails.

Spirit's sacred art,
Heart's peace, balance found within.
Wellness fuels our souls.

Spiritual Fuel

Oh women, it's time to take control,
The transition of change and expansion of soul.
With mercy and resolve, we take the lead,
Harnessing our power, fulfilling our own needs.

Understanding our bodies, a vital key,
Connecting to the inner heartbeat of thee.
Through knowledge and insight, we navigate,
Unveiling the magic, our bodies dictate.

Managing stress becomes a sacred art,
Finding stability and peace in beating hearts.
With healthy choices, nourishing our soul,
Fueling our bodies, making wellness our goal.

In the realm of bonds, strength we embrace,
Sisterhood's love, a comforting space.
Through this mystical passage we tread,
Holding hands, this awareness spread.

With courage and determination, we accept,
The power within, our essence well kept.
Menopause becomes a chapter of renewal,
A time of empowerment, a spiritual fuel.

Bridge the gap with care,
Dismissive views no longer.
Let's educate all.

Dismissive Views

In a world of apathy, healthcare unaware,
Menopause, a burden women must bear.
Voices stifled, our struggles dismissed,
The stigma persists, leaving hearts ensnared.

Dismissive attitudes, oblivious, unprepared,
Medicine faltering, failing to truly care.
But in this battle, education is our tool,
To bring awareness and empathy to the air.

Unshared burdens, carried in silent despair,
Ignorance prevails, leaving women impaired.
Yet we shall rise, united and empowered,
Breaking through barriers, we won't be snared.

We rise, advocating strong and declared,
Shattering fallacies, with knowledge repaired.
Let's bridge the gap, with support displayed,
Changing the landscape, a world more aware.

In this call to action, the tune is clear,
For menopause education, we must steer.
Together we stand, breaking down walls,
Empowering all women, dispelling the fear.

Hormonal shifts stir,
Release stagnant energies.
From ashes, emerge.

Phoenix Rising

Menopause, a rising of the phoenix's flight,
A journey through cycles, from darkness to light.
Sensations awakened, memories may ignite,
As hormones loop, reaching new heights.

Shifting energies stir, from deep within,
Long-held core wounds yearn for a break-in.
Embrace every feeling, let courage be seen,
In stillness, uncover what has always been.

Root causes unearthed, patterns now clear,
Inner work calls, releasing what we fear.
Sitting with feelings, resistance falls away,
Transforming energy, finding peace each day.

Hormonal currents stir the depths of our soul,
Thick and heavy, seeking relief to bring us whole.
A vital relationship with self, in its rawest form,
With vulnerability, we weather the storm.

As emotions pass, dissolving in their wake,
Menopause's liberation, a new path to take.
Rebirth through the flames, emerging anew,
A path of empowerment, a trip for me and you.

In this diamond's sheen, fire's light gleams,
As a parallel course, it merges in fiery streams.
Timelines entwined, collapsing into dreams,
Past and future tap in the now's golden beams.

From ashes we rise, revival's decree,
A symbol of creation, timeless and free.

Self-Mastery Haikus

Embracing wisdom,
Aligned with the higher-self.
Blossom of the soul.

Lifelong Pursuit

In life's boundless quest,

We align with our true self–

Wisdom takes its root.

ESOTERIC WISDOM

In wisdom's deep realm,

Higher self-whispers, guides me–

Divine essence wakes.

DIVINE DESIGN

Fractal nature's art,
Blueprint echoes through the stars–
Galaxy takes form.

ROLE OF CONTRAST

Contrast reveals all,

Source reflects through every form–

We are light's pure truth.

Wonderous Flow

A vibration flows,
Through dimensions, ebbs, and glows–
Consciousness unfolds.

Downward Spiral

Wholeness fractures deep,
Separation from love's core–
Suffering takes hold.

Feedback Loops

Through loops of feedback,
Emotions reveal our state–
Judgement shapes our fate.

SEPARATION'S THRALL

Mind weaves untold tales,
Born from threads of division–
Unity concealed.

Our Heart's Opus

Love's architects craft,

Opus of dedication–

Soul's beauty unveiled.

SPACE-TIME ACTIONS

Observe, let go,
No karmic trace left behind–
Release, choose the now.

Lower Vibrations

Locked centers dim light,

Weary spirits on slow waves–

Seek wisdom, vibe high.

Ego's Grasp

Is the universe

A grand mathematical

Equation of life?

Soaring

In love's grasp we rise,
Shedding masks, we heal, unite–
Sky-bound, whole, we soar.

Mirror of Dreams

Innocent hearts rise,

Compassion blooms, love breaks through–

Universe mirrors.

SHADOW'S FLEETING SHOW

Within my being,
Higher self and shadow blend–
Truth's dance harmonized.

Eternal Presence

Shackles fall away,

Future's uncertainty fades–

Liberation's call.

Guilt's Lessons

Guilt's lessons we learn,
Self-realization dawns—
Divinity shines.

Servants of Love

Love's servants tip scales,
Higher realms where magic gleams–
Souls trust their strong vibe.

Awakening Insight

Puzzle piece denied,
Unity defies ego–
No victims in sight.

TOOL FOR LEARNING

Labels sow discord,

Choose love's path, foes turn to friends–

Peace resounds, oneness.

Inversion of Truth

Unlearn, remember,

Essence whispers in stillness–

Enlightenment blooms.

Illusion of Time

Time's grasp relinquished,
Death's chains lose their strength and fade–
Eternal truth shines.

Reality's Mirror

Universe complete,
Ego indulges in contrasts–
Attachments released.

Cosmic Serenity

Interconnected,
Universal laws guide all–
Karma's balance reigns.

INTERTWINED IN DIVINE

Spirits' fingerprints,

Connected, existing in hue–

Oneness reveals all.

STATE OF BEING

Consciousness, pure joy,
Body's laughter sets us free–
Manifesting dreams.

DIVINE POTENTIAL

Purification,
Awareness lifts the veil—
Karma's ties dissolve.

Quiet Depths

Silent introspect,
Witnessing thoughts as they pass–
True self finds its home.

Love's Frequency

As consciousness soars,

Our spirits dance in the light–

Peace, bliss resonate.

Passionate Presence

Sacred union's grace,
Embrace the gift, souls align–
Awakening truth.

Harmony's Sonata

Hearts awaken, soar,
Love's sonata we explore–
Green ray's guiding call.

ROOT'S MIGHT

Fear blocks our core key,

Healing, freedom, we seek peace–

Root strong, pure, secure.

SACRAL FLOW

Water's ebb and flow,

Sacral's passion starts to grow—

Creativity.

Taking Action

Self-worth and vision,
Engage, golden start unfolds–
Action, sovereignty.

Heart's Stargate

The heart, a portal,
Bridging worlds, helping us blend–
Compassion ignites.

Throat's Broadcast

Truth flows from our lips,
Vibrational waves pulsate–
In the throat, we're free.

Radio Transmitter

Perceive etheric,

Third-eye opens mystic realms–

Intuition's guide.

Field of pure love shines,
Crown guides us to heavens high–
The mystic leads.

Blissful Fragrance

Bliss, Source's nature,
Abundant, infinite grace–
Fear can't touch our souls.

Victim Perception

Transcend victimhood,
Co-create with power and light–
Freedom in realms bright.

Polarity's Balance

Polarity's jive,
Balance of dark and light's stance–
Wisdom through contrast.

Fear's divisive force,
Love's unifying embrace–
Polarity's swirl.

DIVINE INTELLECT

Self-awareness,

Grand design, powers combined–

Realms of intellect.

Sweet Melody

Celestial song plays,
Giving, receiving in tune–
Oneness, grand glow.

Universal Wealth

Transient vessel's guise,
Wealth lies within, soul's treasure–
Abundance unveiled.

INFINITE ABUNDANCE

Lack fades, scarcity
Ceases its thieving, dissolves–
Abundance takes hold.

Human Experience

Birth vessel of life,
Human experience blooms–
Higher self awaits.

Co-Creators

Tales within unfold,
Ascension's gradual path–
Creators we stand.

Heart Field Limericks

I love the mountains
That still the storm's roar,
Where constellations
Crescendo in silent might.
Above the glacier's
Cool, majestic height,
Echoing a blissful
Resonance of light,
With another realm,
Where dreams take flight.

Within my heart's chambers,
Blissful tales unfold,
Where golden age echo's,
Guiding senses are bold.
A melody arises,
Bell's sweet chime,
United in perfect rhyme.
Harmony surrounds,
Life's a joyful ballet,
In the plasma light waves,
Peace it engraves.

Beneath the cherry
Blossom's veil,
I'm lost in a dream,
In the soft whisper of
The evening's gentle stream.
A Zen moment, where nature's
Beauty does gleam,
I'm connected to it all
As one it would seem.

Imagine a tree,
Oh, so proud,
With blossoms so bright,
Fruit growing in sight,
Its beauty radiates
Among the crowd.
Fall colors then fade,
Winter's chill repairs,
But with sunshine,
It stands tall and unbowed.

Our minds, they whisper
Secrets of deceit,
And trust, once firm,
Now falters starts to fade.
In endless circles,
Footsteps we repeat,
A suspicious dance,
Where hope and joy evade.

When misaligned.
We feel discomfort, our stride,
Triggers reawaken
The unity inside.
Motivated as vessels of light,
For a higher reality's might,
Harmony flows when
True essence is our guide.

Oh, how I cherish
My daughter's eyes,
Her soul is magic
That defies,
All worries and pain.
I'm overwhelmed
With pure love again,
In her gaze,
All my troubles subside.

Reconnect unto
The soul's true call,
Create a life where
Harmony holds sway.
For in thy heart,
There's a cure for all,
The doubt that modern
norms are imposed each day.
Embox thy gift of intuition,

Let its wisdom guide,
To find joy where
Purest truths abide.

Speak with integrity, it's clear,
Avoid gossip, lend no ear,
Act with honor, day and night,
Excogitate truth, love's light,
And let wisdom always steer.

All life doth shimmer and gleam,
In shades where shadows
And light team.
The visible and unseen,
Summoning union serene,
In silence, we vanish
The turmoil is within.

The fleeting murmurs
Through the ages glide,
Concealing wisdom
In their hushed embrace.
Yet in the silent dark,
They still abide,
Eternal whispers,
Time cannot erase.
In furtive shadows,
Knowledge shall remain,
A treasure for the few
Who dare to seek.

Besotted by the shapes
That softly call,
The mind doth wander
Through a realm unknown.
In curves and angles,
Wisdom's gentle thrall,
Reflections of our consciousness are shown.
In polar hues
Our hearts reside,
Where tumult reigns
And unity doth lack.
The soul, a tempest
None can e'er abide,
Pays dearly for its peace
With a heavy tax.
In shallow whims
And choices, errant led,
We cheapen truth
With falsity imbued.

Let's hearken the solstice,
Bright and grand.
When day and night emerge,
And nature's splendor
Graces all the land.
The golden rays alight
On fields and trees,
A tapestry of warmth
In light arrayed.

The harmony is fleeting
In moments played.

Does the bird critique
The flower as it sings,
In the morning's light,
'neath heaven's
Golden beams?
Or doth it praise with
Notes on tender wings,
The vibrant hues
That dance in sunlit dreams?

Of fractured souls
Adrift in cosmic seas,
Two spirits wander
Through the void of night.
In timeless dance,
As stars weave destinies,
Their silent cries echoed the light.
They float through ether
On a fated course,
With magnet's pull,
In darkness they do find.

Though tempests rage,
Time may wane & wend,
Our bond is strong
As diamond's gleam.
No force on earth

Such purity can rend,
For we are one,
As one doth flow a stream.
A divine spark ignites,
Drawing my love near,
To magnetize my #soulmate,
That's pure and clear.

I yodel forth my voice
Across the peak.
The mountains echo back,
A wild encore,
As nature's grand cathedral
Hears me speak.
The alpine air, so crisp,
My lungs embrace,
With every note,
My heart feels so free.
A serenade to the sky
And towering tree.

Years have flown
On wings of bitter winds,
And carried with them
All my hopes and fears.
In endless night,
My restless spirit spins,
An emotional vortex
Of sterling tears.
Yet in this darkness,

Light may still arise,
A bloom reborn
Beneath forgiving skies.

In shadows where
Thoughts often hide,
Dormant feelings
Within us abide.
In the corners of
Peripheral mind,
They're hard to unbind,
Whispering truths
We can't quite deride.

The black and white
Of shaded words meld,
A language birthed
In balance, dark and light,
Where silence loud,
And speech in quiet held,
Reflects the human
Soul's eternal fight.
In the lingo of art,
Duality reveals,
The woven truths
That time alone conceals.

A librarian of fate
And destinies,

She weaves the threads
Of stories yet begun.
In silence,
She deciphers mysteries,
Beneath her care,
The timeless rivers run.

A Willow's spirit
Appeared in my dream,
With a spring in its roots,
Majestically did gleam.
But to free this great source,
Called for sacrifice course,
Teaching unity's strength,
And to thrive in esteem.

In a blistering slough
The shadows entwine,
Desire and dreams
In the mire decline.
Yet from this hole,
Where all seems grim,
A spark of light may pierce
The darkened shroud,
As phoenix rises
From the ashes dim,
So too can hope
Emerge from sorrow's cloud.

In the velvet cloak
Of midnight's shroud,
I search for thee,
Amidst the silent stars.
For thy diurnal cycle's shifted,
Another course is now unbowed,
Yet my love for thee endures,
Despite such reckless scars.

My heart's silk element
Of devotion so pure,
Curtain of pain drawn,
Thoughts darken lintel's lure.
I draw them close,
Let shadows softly hide,
Where cherished
Moments abide.
But nature plays songs,
Calm and deep,
And the veil of ice
Begins to seep.

The earth, a living canvas
'neath my feet,
Her body landscapes
Ever-changing form,
Through turmoil and peace,
In tempest or heat,
She whispers secrets
In each fiery storm.

With nature's grasp,
I find reflection,
In this bower where
Flora doth reside.

Through seasons' change,
The stream calmly glides,
A constant thread
In life's eternal weave.
It murmurs soothe where
Restless hearts confide,
In riparian dreams,
The weary find reprieve.

When fleeting hours
like shadows swiftly pass,
And days dissolve
Into the night's embrace,
The ethos of time we glimpse
Through crystal glass,
A tale of transient moments
Etched in cosmic space.

Amid our societal wrangling,
Hope blooms, our collective
Hearts tangling.
With eyes set
On the archaic truth,
We bid farewell to

The loss of our youth,
Breathing out suffering,
Our spirits are untangling.

In Bali's lush
Archipelago space,
Magic seems to
Lace with grace.
Rice terraces cascade,
A verdant spread,
Jungles teem with life,
Where dreams are led.
Mountains rise,
Majestic and grand,
In this enchanted land,
Nature's beauty
And spirits are fed.

In springtime,
the world finds its grace,
As nature paints
Life's vibrant face.
With blooms and with bees,
The rebirth of love
takes place,
In this wondrous,
Verdant embrace.

Upon twilight's canvas,
In nature's sight,

There's a circle
Of aster delight,
Where rolling waters
Compose tales,
Under moonlight's
Soft gales,
Each droplet speaks,
A verse in liquid rhyme,
As currents carry tales
Through the dark night.

In lilac skies where
The stars softly hum,
A tango of lights
It has finally begun.
Boreal winds
Meet the solar air,
In a magnetic affair,
Where marvelous
Celestial magic's spun!

Within the glass,
My soul finds its abode,
A sanctuary for
The wandering mind,
Where secrets dance
In shadows, freely strode,
And solace in its depths,
One seeks to find.
Oh, soul's mirror,

Thou art a sacred art,
Revealing truths
That lie inside the heart.

In a world where
Polarities play,
Opposites dance
In their own way.
Positive, negative,
They like to sway,
In an electric display,
A saga of balance
They portray!

Alone I stand,
My truth in sight,
Ghosts of memories,
Shadows of light.
I muster strength,
With the courage to find,
Through chaos,
A tempest of mind.
I align with my soul,
In search of my might!

Acknowledgment

I want to express my heartfelt gratitude to all the awakened souls on the path of the teacher who also mirror the student within. Their transformative words illuminate our journeys. Delving into their insights on conscious evolution has profoundly changed my life. The light bearer and star seed soul tribe ignite a deep spark within me, fueling my spirit with a sense of belonging and shared purpose. They echo the depths of my inner world, reminding me of our interconnectedness in this existence on a daily basis.

I encourage you to explore the esoteric wisdom from the Alchemist herself, Sarah Elkhaldy; the nature of noetic sciences and modern philosophy with Gabriella Kovalenko; the human origin story and quantum physics through Gregg Braden; the mysteries of ancient geometry with Robert Edward Grant; the teachings on the Law of One and spiritual intelligence from Aaron Abke; as well as insights from The Holistic Psychologist and Dr. Nicole LePera's Self Healers Circle, along with the love revolution wisdom shared by Matt Kahn.

I am profoundly grateful for the insights they share on social media, which resonate deeply with my inner wisdom. Their YouTube content has been incredibly enriching, and I highly recommend exploring their work if these concepts speak to your soul.

About the Author

Lali A. Love is a versatile author whose work spans multiple genres, including dark fantasy, science fiction, paranormal thrillers, and metaphysical poetry. With acclaimed titles such as "Heart of a Warrior Angel" and "The De-Coding of Jo" series, she has garnered a loyal following for her gripping storytelling and uplifting verse.

Her literary repertoire also includes the inspiring coffee table artbook "The Joy of I.T.", the evocative poetry collection "Organic eMotions", and the self-growth transformative poetry series "Realms of My Soul".

In recognition of her gripping storytelling, Lali has received numerous awards, including the NYC Big Book Award, Independent Press Gold Award, the Queer Indie Gold Awards, and International Reader's Favorite Gold Awards.

Her mission extends beyond writing; as an intuitive, alchemist, and energy healer, she aims to empower readers and raise consciousness through her work. Lali advocates for mental health, self-love, authenticity, innocence, and unity, aiming to uplift and enlighten readers worldwide.

With a dedication to bridging metaphysical concepts and captivating writing, Lali A. Love enchants audiences through her thought-provoking narratives and powerful poetry. Her distinctive blend of genre-bending fiction and profound verse inspires, activates, and entertains, providing readers with an immersive experience that transcends the confines of traditional literature.

www.ingramcontent.com/pod-product-compliance
Lightning Source LLC
Chambersburg PA
CBHW052129070526
44585CB00017B/1758
* 9 7 8 1 6 4 7 0 4 9 2 4 9 *